CORNISH PRELUDE

Cornish Prelude

DENYS VAL BAKER

WILLIAM KIMBER · LONDON

First published in 1985 by
WILLIAM KIMBER & CO. LIMITED
100 Jermyn Street, London SW1Y 6EE

ISBN 0-7183-0585-X

Photoset in North Wales by
Derek Doyle & Associates Mold, Clwyd
and printed in Great Britain by
Biddles Limited, Guildford, Surrey

Contents

Introduction

by
Jess Val Baker

The three most important things in Denys Val Baker's life were his writing, his beloved family, and *Sanu* his boat. This latter was nicknamed 'his mistress' by his wife and family and his writing about his adventures sailing her and about his family life soon became compulsive reading for his thousands of fans. Through him, they found that they could escape from their own routine everyday lives, and sometimes even feel inspired to uproot themselves and settle in his lovely Cornish countryside.

He himself was an only child, and as such, often suffered loneliness, so his family were all important to him. He loved having the children around him, planning excursions and outings, or just simply making up a huge picnic lunch for eight, to carry out to them on Porthmeor Beach or pack for some winding cliff walk.

He was deeply involved in the whole process of their upbringing and from early on in our marriage he did more than his share of the endless domestic chores that looking after six children entailed. He would spend hours rocking a baby to sleep, or patiently feeding a toddler. Bath time was his special delight, full of laughter and splashes and rosy slippery bodies shouting with glee, while everything got very, very wet.

He was never strict but endlessly patient, encouraging each child to explore its environment. Perhaps because his own childhood was restricted and lonely he seemed determined that his children would leap from one adventure to another. To Denys everything was possible, money or no money; it was the will that mattered and this philosophy, coupled with a sublime optimism that something would turn up to help him achieve his aim, coloured his whole outlook.

His love for his family gave him a strength to enjoy life to the full and to ride through every trauma that life threw in his way including the many real storms that he encountered in his boat. Denys's navigation was by pure instinct, but he reached every destination with an accuracy that forever astounded us on the voyage through life and the voyage at sea that he took us on.

This is a book about that voyage, about that family, about those children. It attempts a portrait of each child as an individual set in the broader canvas of the whole. Each member is very different, two with different natural fathers, one with a different natural mother, each with their own unique characters their own hopes, their own fears, yet still in some deep hidden, perhaps unconscious way, forever bound together by their united childhood experience and their deep love for a very loving father.

As in all families differences rise to the surface on occasions, but underneath rarely expressed, perhaps inexpressible, lies the bond that is the family, that formed and moulded them and still unites them. Denys formed and cemented that bond and was the strongest element in it. It can never be broken.

J.V.B.

Part One

Characters
in Order of Appearance

I

Martin

When my son Martin was three years old he and I emigrated from the lush wooded countryside of Buckinghamshire to the wilder, more romantic cliffs of Cornwall. I don't suppose Martin remembers a great deal about this period, but for me it is a timeless epoch engraved forever on the memory. My first marriage was at an end, all the nice familiar certainties of life had vanished beneath quicksands, and one of the few verities left was the tremulous relationship with this small but sturdy, curly-haired boy who appeared almost inordinately shy with everyone else but at least, thank goodness, seemed ready enough to put his tiny warm hand trustingly in my own.

In this manner we had managed to sustain the ups and downs of brief periods at my mother's home in Surbiton, then my aunt's farm near High Wycombe, finally within the gracious sanctuary of a Georgian-housed progressive school at Great Missenden. At last I had been able to cut clean all the old bonds: had come to an amicable arrangement that Martin should spend term-time with me, and holidays with his mother; and was all set for a new life in the land of Tristan and Iseult and numerous other ghostly figures.

The way west was a long one, nearly three hundred miles, and I had arranged to spend a night with a friend Malcolm Elwin, biographer and literary critic, who lived in a lovely rambling white house on the edge of the flat sands of Westward Ho. In those days I owned a very ancient Austin Seven saloon, and with all my worldly belongings bursting the seams of the little car, and piled high upon the roof – plus an eager-faced little boy half hanging out of the side window – I suppose we must have made a rather piquant sight. At any rate both

Malcolm and the rather familiar white-haired country gentleman with him appeared very intrigued as they bustled around helping me to unpack.

Over the years I have lost touch with Malcolm but not with his friend, who turned out to be Henry Williamson who was just then beginning his epic series of novels, *An Ancient Chronicle of Sunlight*. At every annual conference of the West Country Writers' Association I always bump into Henry looking younger and younger as, according to the record books, he actually gets older and older, and sooner or later he always remembers vividly that bright spring afternoon when Martin and I arrived. I think, as father of a large family himself and also by then separated from them and his wife, he was curiously touched by the slightly forlorn imagery of father and son embarking into the unknown.

In fact I don't think Martin or I felt particularly forlorn, there was too much that was new and exciting awaiting our attention. After a homely evening at the Elwins, eating a huge supper in front of a roaring log fire and later, with Martin tucked away in bed, relaxing in the immense booklined walls of Malcolm's study I felt full of immense energy and purpose, as if sensing that in Cornwall my writer's imagination would soon be jolted into action. Although this would be Martin's first venture to England's most westerly county, I had myself made a few tentative journeys already, to spy out the lie of the land. I had worked for a short time with repertory theatre companies at Camborne and Falmouth, and later lived in solitary grandeur in a small castle at Portquin on the North Coast, where huge seas pounded frustratedly round the rocky cliffs below ... I had, too, visited the art colony at St Ives long enough to sense that in general the social atmosphere was going to be a pleasant one.

But at first, too, it was going to be a very business-like one. I had managed to rent a tiny cottage way up on the side of Trencrom Hill, overlooking most of Penwith, from Zennor to Godrevy, in the north and from Hayle to distant St Michael's Mount in the south ... and now, bumping down the winding farm track, the tiny Austin brought Martin right to the door of his first home in Cornwall, which was in fact a converted cow-shed.

I needn't have worried much about the reception, for like any boy, Martin was immediately fascinated by the quaint cottage and its country surroundings. It wasn't long before he had settled in to the new life, getting up quite early to wander down to the Triggs' farm and get our daily two pints of milk almost straight from the cow. And after all, what a marvellous setting for a young boy! Trencrom Hill itself, that fabled home of the giants, rearing up in massive protest to the sky … what magical hours we spent wandering about the top ledge, strewn with ancient boulders (supposed to have been used in a game of quoits between the giants of Trencrom and St Michael's Mount).

Sometimes, too, I would take Martin for a walk in the late evening to the lonely top, just to enjoy the fabulous view as the lights came on all over West Cornwall – though to tell the truth once darkness fell we were glad enough to wend our way down again, to the bright oil-fired lamps of Barn Cottage, for a last hot cup of chocolate before turning in for the night.

For nine months Martin and I lived a settled, routine kind of life up at the Barn Cottage. It was not, however, by any means a remote one, for every day saw much coming and going. The day began with us waking up to the sound of Mr Trigg's cows mooing plaintively as they wandered past – sometimes indeed one of them might poke a bovine, inquiring head through the doorway. Perhaps this was prompted by stirrings of dim distant memory, for Barn Cottage really had once been a cowshed, and its simple lay-out consisted of a long living room on one floor, and an equally long bedroom on the top floor. Martin and I slept in two old-fashioned iron bedsteads, and when we woke up in the mornings we simply tumbled down a kind of ship's ladder type of stairway, and while Martin went off to get the milk, I stoked up the Courtier and then lit the calor gas cooker and began making a quick breakfast.

At about a quarter to nine I went out hopefully to start up the old Austin – hope being an operative word, for in the cold weather its record was not too good – and then I drove Martin down to Lelant and on to Carbis Bay, to a small private kindergarten school run by a lady painter with the rather grand name of Miss D. Alicia Lawrence. As was only to be expected Martin's first reaction to this new venture was to clutch my hand grimly and refuse to cross the threshold, let alone participate in corporate life ... but after I had stayed patiently one or two mornings he soon became fascinated with all the activities. Before long he was an eager pupil who ran out of the car on arriving and never spared me another thought.

I was then able, as planned, to drive back to the cottage, make myself a second cup of coffee and settle down at my typewriter for the rest of the morning, and part of the afternoon. I often think that must have been the most prolific nine months of my writing life. Short stories and articles positively poured off the typewriter. I even wrote a complete novel, inspired by the weird setting of Lelant Beach and Hayle Towans. Unfortunately, like one or two other novels I wrote with a Cornish setting, this one did not find a publisher: fortunately the short stories did; the BBC in particular seemed to take a whole sequence of stories. While this did not earn any great amount of money it was good for the ego, for people were always stopping me in the street of St Ives and saying, 'I heard your story yesterday,' as if somehow it had come from outer space.

St Ives was our nearest town, as well as being a beautiful and picturesque fishing port and a famous holiday resort, so naturally enough we tended to spend much of our spare time there. Most days, at least during the spring and summer months, when I picked Martin up from school in the early afternoon I would drive on down Tregenna Hill into St Ives, park the car somewhere, and taking Martin by the hand trundle cheerfully off to one of the beaches. I soon found out that Porthminster Beach was for the visitors, the harbour, too, and that the locals' beach – i.e. the best beach – was Porthmeor, and so it was to Porthmeor, the big surfing beach, that Martin and I would usually make our way.

Of course I had no idea then that one day we would actually live right on the beach, in the form of an increasingly large family unit: but ironically enough, we did even then quite frequently visit what was eventually to be our home. St Christopher's, the name by which it was known then and which we retained when we took over, was then a thriving restaurant run by an elderly couple, the Keeleys. Mrs Keeley was renowned for her home cooking, and every now and then Martin and I would wander in from the beach and stuff ourselves with wholemeal scones, home-made cakes, fresh cream and strawberries – the lot. And yet the price for all this was a mere 2s.6d or 12½p.

The walls of the 65-foot restaurant were adorned with numerous original paintings by St Ives artists (many of them acquired in settlement of long overdue bills, I fancy), and often, so too was the restaurant itself adorned by the presence of many of these artists – Sven Berlin, Peter Lanyon, Patrick Heron, Guido Morris, Bryan Wynter, a whole host, mainly of the younger more modern artists, with whom I found I had most rapport. Martin, in any case an extremely shy boy, always kept very much in the background at these encounters, yet his child's imagination must have been influenced by the constant contact with the arts, and it is not insignificant that later he chose art as his subject and went off to Falmouth Art School.

Our visits to St Christopher's, however, were spasmodic, and most of the time we spent among the rocky pools around the foot of the Island, at one end of Porthmeor. Here Martin and I discovered an affinity in our mutual fascination for rock climbing and exploring pools, and watching the raging sea crashing on distant points. Neither of us were at all interested in swimming then. I could well remember the torturous lengths I had gone to in my own schooldays to avoid visits to the baths, and I did not imagine, now that I had attained the great age of thirty, that I would ever break this pattern.

Ten years later, however, I became so fascinated with surfing that I did slowly begin to venture forth into the sea, and though I hardly ever really mastered the basic technique of swimming I did summon up enough courage to become a reasonably adept surfer, consoling myself always with the somehow comforting thought that the surfing wave was heading in the right direction, shorewards (though a lot of uncomfortable things could happen to you before you were finally washed up half-drowned on the gritty white sands). But for Martin the pattern has never been reversed; he has always resolutely refused ever to go into the water – though, paradoxically, he has spent a good deal of time on the water; whether aboard our MFV *Sanu* or rowing a small blue dinghy down the wide swirling waters of the River Fowey, he has become something of an old man of the sea.

A certain touch of elderliness has always been a feature of Martin's character, even at such an early age as the one I am now describing. The settled routine was as much Martin's choice as mine. He clung ferociously to regular patterns, to set hours of doing things, the same habits day after day – and while some of this was obviously a security thing, some of it was also simply part of his character. He has always been a slightly apprehensive boy, weighing up matters very cautiously, and advancing only with the greatest foreboding and apprehension (paradoxically enough, when under the influence of the demon drink, Martin's character changes quite dramatically and he can be seen dancing wildly, whirling around, doing things which would be unthinkable when sober).

But of course the later times of his favourite pints of keg, beer or whisky and orange were far away from those three-year-old days, and so during our curious secret life together at Barn Cottage Martin's propensity for keeping excessively to himself had plenty of play. He was not, for instance, likely to encourage any of my friendships, particularly with the opposite sex. I never forgot an evening, hilariously amusing in retrospect but heavily embarrassing at the time, when I brought back Elly, a statuesque and really delightful Swedish girl journalist whom I had met on holiday. As soon as she entered our private domain Martin went and hid behind a curtain, an anonymous bulging shape whose presence was more formidably felt than if he had joined whole-heartedly in our conversation – which latter, in any case, soon began to dry up dismally under such pressures.

'Martin, this is Elly.'

Silence.

'Martin, come and say "hullo" to Elly.'

Silence.

'Now, don't be silly.'

Silence.

'You're being *very rude.*'

Silence. And more silence. The whole evening, which had been carefully planned with a bottle of wine and some nice food, became such a strain that in the end I ran Elly home early. She was very sweet and rather amused by it all, but somehow I can't help feeling that the stubborn unseen figure of my unwelcoming son cast a lasting blight on our relationship.

However I was to witness the other side of the coin nearly a year later when a girl to whom I had become very attached, and indeed wanted to marry, made it clear to me that she would only do so on condition Martin did not live with us, as she felt it would be unfair to our relationship ... by blind instinct, which I see now reflected the ethics of good sense, I could not agree to such a condition, and that was that. Despite all the swings of modern progressive opinion (and despite even some pretty weighty swipes in the form of traumatic experiences of family life on my own account) I still cling to the idea that children need their parents as much as their parents need their children.

Elly was one of a series of visitors to our little cottage in the wilderness, and fortunately with some of the others Martin seemed more able to relax. He was always very much at home with Lisa, a striking dark-haired artist's model from Lelant with an impish sense of humour. Those were the days when Lisa was one of the heartwarming sights of St Ives, swinging through the cobbled streets with bright flowing dirndl skirt and gay blouse, her long dark tresses tied carelessly in a bangle, and a huge wicker basket slung over one arm, probably on her way to pose for Leonard Fuller or Marjory Maston, or one of the other painters at the rambling studios along Porthmeor beach.

Mind you, Lisa was only one of the many attractions at a time, just after the war, when St Ives was just beginning to burst into full bloom as a major art colony. I look back with nostalgic pleasure to those days when the artists of St Ives were somehow a little more original, and certainly less mass-produced, than today. There was Sven Berlin, the huge half Swedish sculptor with his bristling black hair and sailor's cap, usually to be seen hewing alabaster outside his studio on the Island; Guido Morris, a fragile-looking but exceedingly tough little printer, operating his ancient old Albion press high in an old warehouse overlooking Porthgwidden Beach; the late Peter Lanyon, one of the few Cornish-born painters, alternating his time between producing striking abstract paintings that seemed to burrow deep into the heart of what Cornwall really meant – and fighting pointless and petty feuds with other painters; Bryan Wynter, desending from his eagle's eyrie at the Carn high up over Zennor moors, to take his bird's eye view of the landscape which later would appear on one of his fascinating large canvases; old John Park, whom I often thought of as a little like Gully Jimson, in *The Horse's Mouth,* that lovable old RA, working away into his eighties in his untidy big studio by the wharf – and many others were among a large contingent of painters and writers who gathered at St Ives about the time of our arrival, drawn by the same intangible lure of ancient Cornwall (plus, in the case of the painters, the marvellous white light).

For myself I was more and more fascinated by the whole romantic story of Cornwall and its world of brooding past mystery – if ever I wanted to stir my imagination I only had to take a few paces up to Trencrom to plunge deep into that world of the past. Or drive, as I often did with Martin, out to the lonely Zennor moors, or down to half hidden paths, like the one down to Kenidjack Cove, with its crumbling caves and old mineshafts – or even to Land's End itself, whose craggy lines and wild view past the long-ships to the distant humps of the Scillies somehow survived the indignities of the bizarre huddle of gift shops, hotels and guest-houses. There was something about Cornwall that would never yield up its mysteries, not even to the commercial exploiters, and this was what drew artists, and still does.

Excitedly I would write to my friends 'up country,' as now they seemed to be, and soon there was a steady stream of visits to my little cottage. Dear to me among them were the writers Reginald Moore and Elizabeth Berridge, who had been most kind and sympathetic during the time my marriage was breaking up. I was relieved to find that from the moment they arrived there was no real problem with Martin, as Reginald and he were both games-mad. In no time we had converted the long wooden kitchen table into a surface for ping-pong, and night after night the four of us, augmented sometimes by Lisa, another table tennis maniac, would conduct immense tournaments – a pleasant relaxation after a busy day touring round West Cornwall.

During these daily tours Martin and I conducted our friends to the steep tumbling cliffs of Gurnard's Head, where W.S. Graham, the Scottish poet, lived in a tiny coastguard's cottage – not far from him (it must have been a poet's season!) lived George Barker, David Wright and John Heath-Stubb. We ventured down the winding lane to Porthgwarra, with its hole in the cliffs through which boomed the sound of the sea ... and one memorable afternoon we climbed above Lamorna Cove, and came upon an encampment of local woodcutters, who were living as a community out on the cliffs. I remember from high up we caught a glimpse of some tanned bearded Apollos and one or two lovely nymphs bathing in the rock pools, and Elizabeth Berridge turned to me with a sigh, 'Where else in England is like this?'

I even began to hope I might persuade Reginald and Elizabeth to put their own roots down in Cornish soil. Unfortunately Reginald had a great interest in psychic matters and one or two visits to Trencrom convinced him that there were sinister things around, and he would rather stay clear. Regretfully we saw them off, and Martin and I went back to our solitary life. Truth to tell I never really found it solitary, if only because the responsibility of looking after my son reminded me that I was not alone. Often I would find friends commenting – sometimes adversely though often, I must admit, in rather pleasing admiration – upon my rather strange life, of bringing up a very young child. Today I fancy this would seem less strange, but to me it was never so. Possibly I have a strongly feminine side to my nature, at any rate I really rather *enjoyed* all the seemingly tedious business of looking after Martin, mothering him, seeing to his clothes, cooking meals; generally, I suppose you might say, fussing.

Of course it is easy to see that I, too, was compensating for some loss – but does it really matter, so long as there is love and understanding? It was regrettable, indeed, that Martin had been deprived of a normal family life, but since it had to be, then the arrangement of his spending part of the time with me and part with his mother seemed quite reasonable. Indeed as the years went by Martin slipped comfortably into the way of life of having two homes without any apparent serious effects. When later on we were settled at St Ives he commuted effortlessly between there and his mother's home at Mevagissey, enjoying both the more sophisticated life of the one and the romantic world of Heligan Woods and Pentwean beach.

It was while Martin and I lived up at Barn Cottage that I began to plan the *Cornish Review,* that extra appendage of my life which has hung around, rather like an extra spoiled child that has never quite grown to manhood, ever since. I had met so many writers and painters and other people busily creating that it began to seem to me a crime there was not a printed vehicle for their views and ideas. Up there in the lonely little cottage on the side of one of the most Cornish of all the Penwith hills I would sit up late night after night writing letters to possible contributors and supporters, while in the bed above Martin slept peacefully. He was too young really to know what it was all about, though I remember he did get a strange excitement about travelling around in our Austin 7 in its gaudy new coat (I painted it white and blue and drew a map of Cornwall on one side, with the title CORNISH REVIEW boldly painted across).

Many years later in the days of the second *Cornish Review* Martin used to deliver consignments for me in his old Bedford Van, so in a curious way he alone of the family has known the *Review* from end to end. Indeed when I think about those early days the picture that comes to my mind is often of the little blue and white Austin parked somewhere like alongside Newlyn fish market or on Mousehole quay, with Martin's bright shining boy's face peering out of the open window, watching all the activity with fascination ... while I went off to call on someone who might somehow be tempted to advertise in our magazine.

Like most sons (indeed my own experience was the same) Martin inevitably developed a kind of instinctive father-opposition, though never, I am happy to say, in a wanton way.

Thus, though his mother and I were both enthusiastic believers in nature cure and vegetarianism as a way of life, and Martin was initially brought up on these lines, as soon as he was able to assert his own wishes, he deserted to the flesh-pots, and subsequently out of all our family, has become the most die-hard meat-eater, cigarette smoker and so on …

I am sad about this but have never attempted to persuade him otherwise, for one of the few but great and cardinal truths I have learned in life is that you can take a horse to the water but you cannot make him drink if he doesn't want to. I personally hold quite a few unpopular views (which of course I believe to be right and progressive!) but with the possible exception of pacifism, which seems to me an essential if we are to save the world destroying itself, I have always tried to avoid thrusting my ideas of what is right upon other people.

Afterwards, as part of a bigger and bigger family circle, Martin and I were to live out on the cliffs near Land's End, in that marvellous old vicarage of Father Bernard Walke's at St Hilary, and finally for the longest period of all, in St Christopher's, that long low house with the doors opening daringly (and rashly) on to the white-crested surfing beach of Porthmeor, St Ives. Yet I suppose it is only natural that for myself, because it marked a curious oasis in my life, a breathless period of waiting between one relationship and another, I tend to remember my year on Trencrom with a special affection … and since Martin shared that year with me, just the two of us for most of the time alone with the haunting hills and the intangible memories of the giants of old, it is of that period in our life as father and son I remember most vividly. And I think I cannot recapture it more aptly, nor take leave of it more affectionately, than by remembering the later part of it, when I had transferred Martin to the charming (though doomed) tiny village school of Trevathack, on the other side of Trencrom. There were only about twenty pupils at Trevathack, and just the one teacher, a delightful old lady of the old school, firm but loving. Alas, I have forgotten her name, and she is long since dead, but she had a marvellous way with the children, who all loved and trusted her – even Martin, and that was saying a lot!

And so that is what I remember most poignantly, those bright autumn mornings when, discarding the old Austin, Martin and I would walk hand in hand across the lane and up the steep side of Trencrom, picking our way sometimes with difficulty over mossy boulders and through burnished bracken – sometimes if we were early snatching a few moments to deviate to the very peak for a quick look over to the white splash of Godrevy on one horizon, the murky misty slope of St Michael's Mount on the other – but always, sooner or later, running down the last steep slope towards Trevathack, nestling romantically and delightfully among lush trees and semi-tropical garden plants.

I never went right to the school gates, because anyway the headmistress would be waiting there; I used to give Martin a farewell hug, and then stand by the last stile, watching as he scampered away down the last stretch, perhaps joining up with one or two of his comrades arriving from Trink or Lelant. Usually he would turn and give a last wave, and then disappear without any further thought for me into his daytime world ... while I would turn and take the pleasant walk back along the winding footpath, my mind turning now to my work for the day.

It was indeed a golden time.

II

Gill

Christmas in Cornwall has become a familiar pattern of our family life for the past two decades: a time almost too good to be true, of huge wood log fires, vast meals, hot punch and wine, and above all people, children, grown-ups, dogs, cats, a laughing, happy, generous period, culminating in our one annual Boxing Night Party. But twenty years ago when I faced the prospect of spending my very first Christmas in Cornwall all alone in a tiny cottage on the side of Trencrom (Martin having gone to his mother's for the holiday) I must admit I jibbed at the rather lonely prospect. Instead I fled back to the somewhat illusory companionship of London and the bright lights, using as my excuse an invitation to a big literary party given by the National Book League.

Since that journey was to change my whole life so radically I suppose it is only fitting I have always retained a vivid memory of the occasion – leaving the old Austin at Penzance Station, catching the swish Cornish Riviera express and indulging in a five course luncheon, and spending the rest of the journey busily addressing hundreds of circulars for the *Cornish Review* (in the end the scene resembled a publisher's office rather than a railway carriage and I was, fortunately, left severely alone by other passengers). At Paddington I caught the tube to Leicester Square where I had arranged to meet an old friend, Fred Roskelly, in that marvellous mirror lined actors' pub, the Salisbury.

Here, sinking back into the red plush cushions of the back 'snug' we eagerly exchanged our news and gossip covering the period since we had last been together, when we both worked for a repertory theatre. There was something a little ironic

about Ross, a true-blue Cornishman, now living exiled in
London, while it was left to me, a 'furriner' to bring news of his
homeland. However, I knew that Ross, an extremely sociable
and sophisticated person, really felt at home in the metropolis.
Although he took up odd jobs, like editing a literary magazine
or journalism, Ross's main, almost sole interest, was people
and their destinies. He had an unfailing capacity for making
new encounters and uncovering strange and unusual
characters – and undoubtedly one of the reasons for his success
in this way was an absorbing interest in astrology. He knew
what he was talking about, too: the very first time we met Ross
simply stared at me and declared, 'Ah, Scorpio!' a correct
diagnosis.

So now when, during the course of a very pleasant social
evening, first at the Salisbury and then later, among a crowd of
other young writers, at the NBL's stately home in Albemarle
Street, Ross kept telling me I simply must come and meet a
new friend of his – 'a pretty little Sagittarian, ideal for a
Scorpio, old boy' – I could hardly fail to be intrigued. Later
that evening, when Ross took me round to a flat off Fulham
Road and introduced me to Jess, the 'little Sagittarian' I was
rather more than intrigued.

Just as the astute old astrologer had predicted, we hit it off
immediately. Of course we had many things in common. We
were both Welsh, with all the inbred and intuitive ties of the
Celtic race. We had much the same attitude to life, being what
might be termed humanist socialists – that is we had a
reverence for the dignity of the human being and a belief that
the world should be organised by the people for the people,
and not by a few monopolies and capitalists for their own gain.

On the other hand in many ways we were apparently
opposites (or perhaps, as experience was to suggest,
complementary). Jess was an extrovert, I was an introvert, Jess
assessed people as they seemed, my judgements were arrived at
by a more tortuous caution, an intuitive feeling. Jess made
friends very easily, I could only do so over a long period of
time. Jess was a product of Cardiff University, and a long
history of activity in university debating societies had helped to
make her an incisive and logical and forceful talker. Being a

writer I was much more forceful on paper than in conversation.

Not that I lacked conversational fire with Jess. We often became involved in the most fantastic arguments and wrangles – part of a sparking off process which, I'm glad to say, has continued through all the years. In one sense we were fighting to be free, in another we were weaving the bonds around us ... and all the time Ross sat by nodding approvingly, like a wise old mandarin.

Someone else sat by, too, very pointedly, in those early days of our courtship. Her name was Gillian Elaine, she was three years old (only a few months younger than Martin) and she was Jess's elder daughter by her first marriage – which, like my own, had ended in divorce. There was a younger daughter, too, Jane, but at that time she was staying with a foster parent and so did not then appear on the scene. For one thing Gill was an extremely pretty little thing, with curly blond hair and bright blue eyes inherited from her Norwegian father, and she knew only too well how to make the most of her formidable charms. For another thing – she did not take at all kindly to the appearance on the scene of a possible rival for her mother's affections. I had never courted a mother and child before, and I must say the experience often proved a trying one. The obvious physical manifestations were difficult enough – invariably, if I went to sit beside Jess Gill would run over and separate us, and always if we were out walking, she would insist on walking between us. But there were other more needling ways of intrusion; a fit of tantrums if Jess and I were planning to go out together, a tendency to get lost on outings, and so forth.

I had the sense to realise that these things were inevitable, and had to be not only endured but circumnavigated, but it was a long and exasperating process. On the other hand it must have been exasperating for Gill, too. In the end I guess we both made concessions of various kinds, until at last, finally there began to appear welcome signs of what might be called integration. I think it all dated from one sunny afternoon when the three of us paid a visit to Hampton Court Palace and Gill got lost in the Maze, and finally I found her, all tearful and frightened, and was able to comfort her and return her safely to the maternal fold.

Early in the New Year, only about a month after our first meeting, the little Sagittarian and the solitary Scorpio were married at South Kensington Registry Office in a flurry of agitated relations and friends, the ceremony being followed by a hilarious wedding tea at the Old Blue Cockatoo Cafe on Chelsea Embankment and an evening party at Jess's flat. By now, of course, our two progeny had been properly introduced – a most amusing encounter with Martin arriving full of shyness after his holiday, to be greeted by a Gill all dolled up in her prettiest dress, suddenly and rather untypically struck herself by a bout of shyness.

If we had had any forebodings about this encounter we were soon able to forget them for almost at once Martin and Gill established the relationship which was to persist throughout the whole of our family life – what might be called a live-and-let-live relationship. After all, it made a fair enough balance – Jess and her child, Denys and his child. They were both able to continue to feel both secure and special, and operating from such well established bases soon found plenty in common.

In a short time, to all intents and purposes they had become just like a natural brother and sister, a state of affairs encouraged by the fact that for the first few years of our life together, if only out of economic necessity, Martin and Gill had to share not only life but even the same bedroom together.

Thinking back on what was inevitably a period of great upheaval in our lives, I realised that in the first few months of our married life Gill and Martin's shared bedroom changed environment three times. At first they occupied the only remaining spare bedroom in Jess's flat off Fulham Road, a place already chaotically full of female flat-mates, their boy friends, plus Ross and a few other extraneous objects. I suppose it was the kind of set-up quite common in that area of London, though it all seemed marvellous and unique at the time, with a gaiety and freedom one remembers with special affection.

Jess's flatmates were two very dissimilar girls – Denise, a sultry half-Egyptian beauty (an extraordinary mixture of Roedean English and exotic East), who later married Erik de Mauny, a

lively and sophisticated New Zealand poet who became well
known as a BBC correspondent: and Betty, a Cardiff girl with a
kind heart and a grim determination to find herself a husband
(there were many hilarious evenings when special dinner
parties were laboriously prepared for one of Betty's intended,
all of whom at that time somehow slipped through the noose).
Denise never seemed to get out of bed until mid-day, and spent
a large part of the time languorously draping herself around
the flat looking indeed most ravishing: Betty on the other
hand, like Jess, had a regular job. All three girls led quite
separate lives, yet they managed to remain surprisingly friendly
and quite tolerant of each other's activities.

Thus, when now I moved in for a while with Jess, and what's
more brought a four-year-old son to add to the menagerie, it
was all accepted with good grace – and indeed Denise and
Betty made very useful baby-sitters in those early days of our
married life, when naturally we wanted to get out and about
on our own.

Fortunately, as I say, Gill and Martin found apparent
satisfaction in their own company. Martin, as ever, remained
the shy and fairly withdrawn one, but Gill, once she had lost
her own initial shyness, was soon able to get her way with him
to quite an extent. Every now and then, particularly it seemed
on a Sunday morning when we were all stricken with
hangovers from some Saturday night party, childish mischief
would rear its ugly head. Almost as if sensing our
unwillingness to bestir ourselves Gill and Martin would
embark on fiendish pranks – the most awful of which must
have been (since I remember it with horror to this day) one
Sunday morning when they opened the cases of their pillows
and scattered feathers all over the flat, in every room, every
corner, even among the food in the kitchen – and, of course,
all over Jess and me, sleeping peacefully in the front room (I
am not sure they didn't put sticky stuff on the feathers, and
stick them all over our faces, but this they stoutly deny).

It was a curious beginning to married life in many ways. For
the time being Jess had kept on her job as laboratory assistant
at Glaxo's, at Greenford, in Middlesex, and so every morning
at seven o'clock she was up and about and off on the long tube

journey – leaving me to cope with the two children. We had temporarily enrolled them at the nearest infant school, just off King's Road, and though this was not exactly one of the poorer quarters of London, nevertheless the health record at the school seemed bad, and almost every week there was an epidemic of measles or mumps or something.

I am sure that Martin and Gill got through more than their regular quota of these childish ailments during those three months. I have somewhat bitter memories of endlessly opening doors to doctors, and equal endlessly carrying meals on trays to the 'quarantine' bedroom. As always with children's illnesses it seemed to be the poor parent who ended the day thoroughly exhausted. I know I did, so that by the time Jess arrived back I was thoroughly irritable. As she was probably equally tired from her long day and journey we would often embark upon ridiculous squabbles. Fortunately we realised that circumstances were the cause and were determined as soon as possible to remove ourselves to a healthier part of the world.

In the meantime, socially we continued to enjoy London life, though obviously it was conditioned by now having a family. As a compromise every Sunday we would make an effort to have an outing somewhere – on the River Thames, to Richmond Park, or further afield, out to Esher or Oxshott, a favourite haunt of mine since childhood days in that area. There was something curiously artificial about these outings, I always felt, and already I was planning hard for our removal. My own income as a writer was pretty spasmodic but just about enough to live on if we returned to the cottage at Trencrom. Jess would get some kind of bonus from Glaxo when she left, so there did not seem much point in long delaying the move – especially as it was spring again.

So at last Jess and I gathered together our belongings, including Martin and Gill, and left the hurly-burly of London for the quieter and more romantic fields of Trencrom. The cottage would at least make a convenient base for a while until we could find a more permanent home. Some domestic re-arrangements were now necessary, of course. In effect, Jess and I lived on the ground floor room, and Martin and Gill made their home in the long room upstairs. Like most children they soon adapted themselves to the new environment, and had the time of their lives playing among the granite boulders of Trencrom, or tobogganing down the gorse-strewn sides.

For the couple of terms that we continued to live at Barn Cottage Gill joined Martin at Trevarrack School, and so now there were four of us, instead of two, meandering across the hill. When the sun shone and the sea stretched blue and untroubled to Godrevy Lighthouse it was impossible to wish we were anywhere else. The difference between the high clear air tanged with a scent of the sea and the diesel-laden fumes of London must have an enormous effect on a child's health. And what a marvellous way to start schooling in such an environment; when nature study period came it was simply a question of taking the children wandering down lanes strewn with hawthorn and blackberry bushes or among the near by woods of Lelant Downs.

For Gill, of course, it was all new, and apparently satisfactory – particularly the times spent literally by the seaside. From an early age Gill was a natural swimmer, a reflection in some ways of her character. (Her sign, like Ross's, is Pisces, the fish.) Like all Pisces Gill manages to keep afloat in the maelstrom of life's complications. I can't remember whether she could actually swim in this first year in Cornwall but she was always in and out of the water, trying wickedly to entice Martin in too, but never succeeding. St Ives beaches were naturally one of the main attractions; but also, because much nearer, the weird setting of Lelant Beach and Hayle Towans.

Here a narrow estuary and bar pierces the land pattern, so that we could be lying on the beach and look up to see a strange sight, huge cargo boats gliding past on a level with us, rearing high in the sky, coming in on the tide, when the bar was safely covered by fifteen or twenty feet of water. Most afternoons after school that summer we would pile into the little Austin and nip down to Lelant Church, then walk across the golf links and under the tiny railway bridge and down to where the old man sat patiently waiting with the Hayle ferry boat (now defunct I hear).

I remember reading a charming account by Havelock Ellis of how he and his wife did their courting walking along the Lelant beach to catch the ferry boat over to Hayle, and certainly it was a little world of its own, somehow unaffected by the vast edifice of an electric power station rearing up a little way down the river. Then there was the veritable eyesore of Hayle Towans, a strange encampment of little wooden chalets scattered about the sand-dunes that stretched miles up the coast to Gwithian.

In the winter it was like a ghost town, and then suddenly for a few weeks in the summer busy with activity. Lines of bathing costumes and towels drying on lines outside each chalet ... Despite all this the estuary entrance remained always for us a very strange place. I know for my part it was a setting that continually haunted me.

When we got back to Barn Cottage after such outings the children would run up to their long room to play, while Jess and I busied ourselves with the evening meal. Practical conditions in Barn Cottage, which had never bothered me much, were not quite so popular with my new wife. I was able to feel romantic about a home tucked way down a lane and one and a half miles from the nearest main road, where the only water was obtained in buckets from a stream a hundred yards away, where cooking was done on a Primus or on a ferocious old paraffin stove and lighting was equally dependent on the same fuel, plus the temperament of two Aladdin lamps. For Jess it was a form of purgatory and she reacted accordingly. We had many momentous rows glaring at each other across the inefficient smoking futility of a stove whose wick was burned out or after I had tired of carrying innumerable buckets of water which, it appeared to me, Jess wantonly wasted.

When we had these rows there was a somewhat curious reaction on the part of our rather quickly acquired ready-made family. Instead of, as one might suppose, each siding with their respective parent, they joined to form what I suppose might be called a moderating third force. This was not of course especially self-evident at such a young stage but it was a trend that became well-defined later, and often I can remember, when Jess and I have been involved in some especially childish argument (the way all parents do become involved, say what they like!) Gill and Martin looking at one another and raising their eyebrows expressively, or nodding their heads in bewilderment, as if they were the parents.

Of course our rows did not last long anyway, and one of the surest ways of ending them was for us to notice this superior behaviour on the part of our offspring. They for their part hardly ever seemed to quarrel – indeed I don't think I can remember a single large scale row between Martin, anyway the great tactician, and Gill, the over easy-going Pisces.

Jess and I were only able to stay a few months at Barn Cottage before we moved to the first of many new homes (which expanded as our family expanded), but I think we realised that they were rather precious months, not only for ourselves, but for establishing the family as a whole. True, Martin could be exasperating, Gill incredibly petty and so on, but every day came to its appointed end, and somehow things seemed safer and different at night. Outside all was dark and mysterious – inside there was the peace of the long low room, lit by a cosy stove at one end and the friendly light of the Aladdin on the centre of the long scrubbed table. It was somehow a romantic room at night, even the white-washed walls took on a soft glow.

An hour or so after Martin and Gill had officially gone to bed, and all would seem quiet for some time, we would invariably climb up the wooden ladder and peep at them. Lying there in their two tiny beds – looking incongruous in the huge, long room – they would look infinitely tender and appealing, tucked deep into the bedclothes, We used to creep away down the stairs back to the warm room below and forget all our petty quarrels, thankful for the wonder of being alive and in love, and embarking on such an adventure of life.

III

Jane

During the early months of our marriage Jess and I had thought it wise to concentrate on settling down our newly acquired 'family' one by one, so to speak. So her younger daughter, Jane, remained for a while with foster-mothers in London, this seeming the sensible course to follow while we were coping with the severe restrictions of our two-roomed cottage at Trencrom. When these restrictions finally became too much for us and we started rather desperately looking around for a more permanent home one of our pre-requisites was, of course, that it should be large enough to accommodate not only Martin and Gill, but Jane as well – and for that matter (hollow laughter) any other tiny little V.B.'s that might ultimately arrive.

At last we moved into a large old Georgian house in a quiet terrace behind Morrab Gardens, Penzance. Only a few yards away the buses ran up and down Morrab Road, with its long line of doctors and dentists and guesthouses and, at the top, Penzance Art School; behind us were the offices of *The Cornishman* and sloping away, easy of access, Morrab Gardens themselves, a wondrous place of camellias, magnolias and sub-tropical plants of all kinds – while in the distance, visible from the top floor, stretched the vast waters of Mount's Bay, with the Lizard lighthouse winking in the distance at night time. It was all rather different from the romantic wild country of Trencrom, but I had to admit it was rather pleasant to enjoy some home comforts.

For a time we wallowed in the sheer luxury of space plus the conveniences of constant hot water, electric light and gas cooking. Jess and I lay around lazily in a lovely big Georgian bed-sitting room below, which had an old fashioned coal fire. I made an office for myself and the *Cornish Review* in one of the rear rooms with a somewhat unedifing view of a white-washed back yard (we had no garden, alas), and still there remained four or five rooms higher up …

It was time, obviously, to welcome into the home our third child, and so in due course Jane arrived, blonde like her sister Gill, but with straight hair, not curly. I suppose in a way this marked a significant change in the pattern of our family life. Hitherto there had been some kind of illusion of compactness, of a small unit – why, I remember we even used sometimes to go out for a meal in a restaurant as if it was quite a normal thing. The arrival of a third child somehow heralded an end to this casual kind of approach – henceforward we were moving relentlessly into the 'Big Family,' category, with all the mixture of blessings and draw-backs associated with that generous phrase.

As an only child myself who was eventually to become that stage character, 'father of six,' I am in a position only too well to define the meaning of this sort of phrase. There is a big, total difference between the one extreme and the other. I well remember how being an only child I was able to travel anywhere with my own mother and father, without there being any problems. To travel anywhere with a family of six children is a problem in itself, and only too often one avoids the problem by not doing something rather than face all the awful consequences. Dining out in a restaurant (even assuming one could afford it on such a scale) is an obvious example. The agony and frequently the embarrassment of persuading six children of different ages first to sit relatively still and then to make up their minds about what they want to eat – no, the mere memory of it all brings furrows to my forehead!

It would not be fair to blame Jane in anyway for this, but I think perhaps it was a little unlucky for her that somehow she was associated with the change of status. Also, of course, being the younger sister, Jane felt from the beginning a kind of inferiority to Gill, and this created its own problems. One way and another the early months of Jane's absorption into the family bosom were delicate ones, certainly for her, and often for us. Like all married couples Jess and I found the early months of adjustment difficult enough, and now suddenly with the careful balance of our ready-made family altered, there were ample opportunities for stress and disagreements.

Looking back I can see that even at that early age Jane must have reacted to all this, feeling in some way rather over-conscious of her newness, so to speak. To compensate for any feelings of inferiority, real or imaginary, Jane was wont to indulge in a considerable gift for the dramatic. I do not particularly remember any great dramas with Martin and Gill, but over the early years there were many with Jane. For instance, one of my earliest memories is of the postman calling, and Jane rushing through the house screaming 'The Post! The Post!' just as a distraught person might call 'Fire! Fire!'

Sometimes, of course, there was justification for the sense of drama: once, some years onwards, while playing on Praa Sands, Jane trod on an adder and received a bite. The result was a cliff-hanger, with a car dash to the house of the district nurse, only to find her out, then another mad drive to West Cornwall Hospital, with Jane in a kind of trance, and at last the administration of the special anti-serum. It all seemed to age us a little, and we couldn't help wishing, perhaps unreasonably, that Jane *wouldn't* step on an adder.

I think what I am trying to say, to put it simply, is that Jane is a typical Virgo. Virgos are not created to lurk under bushes, they are natural extroverts, and it is as normal for them to parade their emotions dramatically as it is for another person, i.e. an old Scorpio, to hide them somewhat unnaturally. This tendency to dramatisation is one of the failings of the Virgo. On the other hand they have many very attractive qualities. For instance Jane has always been able immediately to strike up friendships with people. Then a Virgo is never afraid to venture into all kinds of formidable situations without blinking an eyelid.

Another very attractive side to Virgos, and to Jane in particular, is a natural tendency to try and help people. This was noticeable even in these early days of which I am writing: little Jane was always trying to help her new brother and her older sister – efforts, I regret, that were not greatly appreciated. In the somewhat ultra-realistic way of children, Martin and Gill from the beginning tended to form a little front of their own against this intruder ... and so it took a long time for Jane really to settle down.

When she finally did so she became the most family-conscious of all the children, remembering birthdays and other significant events with religious regularity (whereas with all the others it was a case of 'Good heavens, is it *really* your birthday? Well, I haven't any money *just now,* but I won't forget.' Nor would they forget: two, three, perhaps four months later, some strange object would be produced to fulfil the long-forgotten promise).

If she had been just a little older Jane would have revelled in our new life at Morrab Place, for suddenly faced with a financial crisis which my spasmodic earnings from writing could not meet Jess and I had decided to take in lodgers. Or rather to be more precise, to let rooms – I don't think we could have coped with the Cornish way of life, B and B. No, our idea was to let out one or two spare rooms at rents which would cover our mortgage payments and our weekly food bills – so that at least we would never starve or lack a roof.

Of course, things didn't work out quite like that. Either our lodgers turned out to be bosom friends from whom we found it somehow impossible to take the full rent, or else so dislikable that we had to find an excuse to get rid of them, and were left again with empty rooms. One way and another life at Morrab Place was never dull – or so it occurs to me, looking back on a long list, including the prim spinster with the middle-aged lover who called every Tuesday and Friday; the health and efficiency fanatic who spent hours before a full length mirror; the psychiatrist in charge of a problem patient with whom we were only too often left to cope; the delightful eccentric English lady with a passion for the crafts and a genuine feeling for psychic manifestations ... not to mention a sequence of young potters who proved among our most impecunious tenants, but nevertheless were responsible for kindling an interest in pottery on Jess's part which was later to lead her to start her own pottery.

Yes, Jane would have been very much at home in such a set-up, for ever since her early teens she has seemed to gravitate instinctively to the heart of things, taking charge, organising and so on. She is still remembered, I gather with some awe at the Cornwall Technical College where she managed somehow to spend four years mysteriously studying nothing except shorthand-typing, but otherwise giving the impression of single-handedly running the social side of the college. At other times she has moved into people's homes and taken over the running of the house, or the looking after of children, sweeping everything forward with great confidence. On occasions such a self-assurance might lead to some trouble, especially if coming up against someone else self-assured in another direction; but in general it works very well.

I remember for instance halcyon days when being almost the oldest pupil at St Christopher's, a small private school at St Ives, Jane seemed to acquire immense authority; shepherding parties of small children here and there, organizing games, planning outings … It must have come as quite a shock to the headmaster when Jane finally left and he had to cope again all on his own.

Our first lodgers at Morrab Place, Anthony and Dorothy Richards, were to become our friends. Anthony was a neat almost dapper figure of a man, dark-haired and with a carefully trimmed dark beard that made him look rather older than his twenty-eight years. His wife by contrast was a lush Rubensesque type, half Greek by birth and reflecting the Eastern influence in her dark skin and almost jet black hair. We didn't see a great deal of Anthony as every morning he departed at the fantastically early hour of 7 a.m. to catch the early bus out to Lamorna Pottery, where he worked very long hours for a somewhat meagre wage of £7 a week. But Dorothy and the two tiny children were very much present, the latter contributing about another 100 per cent to the noises of the day. What with them and our own children life at Morrab Place was never exactly quiet. Sometimes in the evening we would share a cup of tea together with our new lodgers, whom we liked as simple and unspoiled people, vaguely groping towards some sort of satisfying life, like ourselves.

Unfortunately Anthony's monetary problems soon became our own. With a total wage of around £7 and a family of four to support it was not surprising that Anthony had difficulty in finding even a fairly low rent of 30s. This we quite understood but as things hadn't improved for me we felt the only thing to do was to rent off yet another room ... So our career as landlords expanded. Of course we decided firmly only to let rooms to 'respectable' (i.e. rentworthy) folk, but in the end somehow, as I have mentioned, our household grew into a very bizarre one. We were not, honestly, sorry about this, because this was half the fun of life, meeting and coping with the eccentrics of life.

In all we owned Morrab Place for some five years or so, though in fact our own actual residence there was to prove a surprisingly brief one. Long after we had moved to Sennen Cove, however, we kept the house on let out to tenants, and producing for us a weekly income of incalculable importance. I can remember at this time reading in one of the children's school books an essay on 'How I spend my Saturdays' which began something like this: 'Every Saturday morning we all get in our car and Daddy drives us to Penzance and we collect our rents.' This was a state of affairs of which morally I do not really approve, anyway, but I have to admit that for the short period it endured we were often entirely dependent on those Saturday mornings visits.

My writing was going through a very sticky patch financially, with cheques few and far between, and we were desperately grateful for small mercies every Saturday morning – five small ones in fact, as by now we had let the whole house. With the sort of tenants we had, a happy-go-lucky lot (we did not always use such a polite term) this meant we could never be quite sure we were going to get our rents. I well remember how nervously I would begin each Saturday 'round,' secretly keeping my fingers crossed not only about the rents, but lest some unforseen disaster had befallen, such as a ceiling collapsed, a wash basin cracked, lights fused, furniture burned, gas cooker broken and so forth (all of which happened at one time or another).

In general our tenants were pretty reasonable. No doubt all kinds of odd happenings took place there at one time and another, which fortunately I never knew about, but at least to the end the house remained standing in one piece. Sometimes, I must admit, I was surprised.

Ultimately we fell so behind with the mortgage payments on Morrab Place that the building society announced its intentions of exercising its rights to take over the house. We were faced with the melancholy task of giving notice to our tenants and cutting off about half our income.

Although of course we could not help ourselves, we felt rather like executioners. Our only real problem, it turned out, was going to be Anthony (who by then, alas, was separated from Dorothy). He meant well, of course. Yes, he really must find another place. Yes ... meanwhile he went on living alone, installed on the ground floor, eating, sleeping, reclining on couches, clothes everywhere, no sign of movement.

We began to call round anxiously.

'Any luck, Anthony? Have you heard of anywhere? You won't forget the deadline?'

Immediately Anthony would look worried and apologetic.

'Yes, yes – come to think of it I did hear there was a cottage at Newlyn. It's condemned or something. I might be able to get that.'

A night or two later we would ask eagerly.

'Did you get that cottage at Newlyn?'

Anthony would look most contrite 'Er, well, I've been so busy. I haven't had a chance – But I will call there tomorrow.'

Somehow we could never believe the inevitable would happen, but it did. The appointed date for our vacation of the premises arrived, a fine, falsely happy day, and *still* Anthony remained an installation. The rest of the house was an empty shell, echoing with mournful memories; but the ground floor saw Anthony home for the day, resolutely eating lunch.

'But Anthony, you promised – '

'We've arranged for the furniture to be collected – '

'They'll be coming to cut off the gas – '

'Yes, and the electricity – '

Like a hunted man at bay Anthony went red in the face and brandished a knife and fork.

'I don't care – I can't deal with it now – I want my lunch!'

Afterwards he calmed down and there then ensued an

afternoon right out of a Chekhov play. Anthony's partner, Len, popped in and one or two other friends and we all sat around in Anthony's lounge sharing a bottle of wine.

Soon there was a loud knock at the door, and I jumped to my feet.

'That'll be the electricity, I'm afraid.'

It was, too. Closely followed by the gas. Both armed with orders to cut off their respective supplies.

Fortunately there was a coal grate and although Anthony had no coal there were one or two orange boxes around. We soon had a nice blaze going.

We were just settling down again and solving Anthony's immediate future by arranging that he should join Len at his new digs when there came further arrivals. This time it was a dealer to take away Anthony's bed and couch. He had barely gone when another dealer arrived for the chairs and table. As each article of furniture went so we manoeuvred about, one sitting on the window seat, one on a remaining chair, one on an upturned orange box. Meantime the light was fading and so Len slipped out and came back with some candles. I think also he brought a second bottle of wine.

Then, with all the furniture gone, we all sat on the floor drinking wine by candlelight, almost convulsed with a sort of gay hilarity over the bizarre situation. Maybe it was the wine, or maybe the cosy effects of the candle-light and the fire, but as the evening wore on we became curiously exhilarated … and what was in a way a disastrous day for us somehow momentarily became a slice of life's comic opera. We sat together, a charmed circle, each in turn remembering some facet of the turmoil of life that had filled the house in the past. I often remember that scene by the fire. Symbolic of some golden era when life was often hard and desperately worrying, yet sustained by a communal strength, so that at the worst moments we could always raise a laugh.

IV

Stephen

When Jess and I had completed our first year of married life we celebrated the occasion in doubly dramatic fashion: first, by planning to move from Morrab Place to a remote cottage on the cliffs above Sennen Cove, a mile or so from Land's End itself – and second by adding to our already large family by the arrival of the first child we could truly call our very own, Stephen Roskelly Val Baker, born during a wild winter's night. He weighed over 9 lbs, had a tuft of blond hair and a pair of bright brown eyes and in no time at all was yelling his little head off – possibly to demonstrate his apprehension of the somewhat impoverished family life he had joined.

The two celebrations very nearly coincided, which would have made things even more dramatic – for delivering a baby out at Peter's Cottage, high above the white-crested Atlantic rollers, could hardly have been called a normal event. What happened was that, as Stephen's impending arrival became more and more evident from poor Jess's vast frame and slowing movements, so I became more and more restless about our situation in Penzance. I couldn't suppress a feeling of being stifled by living in the heart of a town. Instinctively I longed to get back to the romantic Cornwall that I had known up at Trencrom.

At least I supposed so. Not long ago I came across an old school essay by Martin about different homes he had lived in: it began quite boldly and perhaps a little sourly. 'For some reason my father was obsessed with a wanderlust.' Perhaps that is true to some extent, though I am not the normal sort of wanderer. I like comfort and routine and am most wary of hazardous expeditions. Still, I must admit I have spent most of the past twenty years either moving house or planning to move house, or alternatively setting sail upon boats for far-flung corners of the world. So perhaps Martin had something.

Whatever the reason or motive, shall we say that I was keeping my eyes open, and through a friend I came to hear about the offer for sale of Peter's Cottage. I have never known whether to be glad or sorry that my first approach was the essentially romantic one, coming over the top slope of the cliffs along a winding tortuous path, to find the grey-slated double fronted cottage almost beneath my feet. For a while I could only stand and stare, lost in admiration at one of the most beautifully situated settings I have ever seen. Other parts of Sennen Cove have arisen haphazardly, often consisting of badly built bungalows and shacks, but Peter's Cottage – all on its own, the very last cottage along a cliff top before the mile walk to Land's End itself – was one of the old style Cornish granite cottages that seem to blend naturally into the Cornish landscape. Several hundred feet beneath the cottage, reached by twisting stone steps, was the village of Sennen Cove itself, mostly built around a tiny harbour and the Sennen Cove lifeboat station.

It was a majestic panoramic view, and I knew at once in my heart that I wanted to live there. Going on down the path and knocking at the door, introducing myself to the owners and being shown over the cottage – that was all a perfunctory going-through-the-motions.

'And what's the lowest you would consider taking?' I heard myself saying suddenly.

It wasn't as simple as all that, of course. First, there was the problem of Jess, who was rather enjoying the convenience of civilised things. Although Peter's Cottage was quite well equipped in the practical matters, being all-electric, I knew that Jess might not fancy such an isolated spot. I could only go back and enthuse as effectively as I could and pray that it would be a lovely sunny day when I took Jess out to see her prospective new domain.

Fortunately it was: the air was full of the scent of honeysuckle and sea pinks and everything looked rather like a scene out of paradise. There was even a lovely sunlit patch of lawn built into the cliff-side where baby Stephen, when he arrived, could sleep all day in his pram ... yes, even Jess's romantic soul, more cautious than mine, was suitably stirred. I was in any case assaulting her at an unfair time, when she was full of the softness and tenderness of expectant motherhood.

'But what about Morrab Place?' said Jess, rather weakly.

'Ah!' I produced my master-stroke. 'That's just it – we'll be able to let out all the rooms. We'll have a regular income!'

These were magic words in Jess's ears, and I saw the last of her real objections vanishing. At any rate she put up no real resistance – a fact, I was to learn later, due more probably to increasingly urgent signs from within that Master Stephen was on the move. Indeed, the very next day after our journey out to Sennen Cove, our new son saw the light of day, in a room high up that terrace house in Penzance.

A very few weeks later we were living out at Sennen Cove, and it is with that wind-swept, sea-scented place that we always associate our first experience of joint parenthood. At Land's End one has to learn to live with the wind and the profusion of damp mists that settle like a plague. But there are compensations, as we began to find out during the next two years.

Once we had settled in at the cottage, and Martin and Gill and Jane were attending the village school at the top of the hill, there was only baby Stephen to worry about. Every morning, after a good feed, he would go off into a deep sleep tucked into his pram parked in the middle of our tiny lawn. Often, about mid-day Jess and I would seize the opportunity to slip out along the cliff path, leaving Stephen peacefully dreaming while we strolled along the short cliff walk to the Land's End point.

These walks were something we would never forget, for during them we became conscious of a tremendous solitude, of being literary alone with the vast universe. Everywhere the cliffs ended abruptly in steep precipices, granite slabbed slopes down to jagged rocks and swirling waters. Rounding the curve towards Lane's End we could see the huddle of odd shaped rocks leading out to the famous Longships Lighthouse and beyond that the Armed Knight, Dr Syntax and several other rock formations to which the guide books have given popular names.

Invariably we would throw ourselves down on the grassy slopes and stare up into the azure sky, while the music of the sea and the seagulls' cries blended harmoniously in our ear, and the scent of seaweed and wild thyme tickled our nostrils. Then came the gentle walk back, this time with quite a different panorama; the huge sweep of White Sand Bay, with the sea travelling across in steady long lines of swell, to pour itself upon the wide golden sands of Sennen, while on the horizon Cape Cornwall, the only cape in England, poked outwards like a humped fist. After a stroll such as this one felt invigorated not merely by the fresh Atlantic breeze but by an awareness of the joy of living itself.

But more invigorating still was the rather comic sight of that tiny blond head struggling to peer round the corner of his pram, awaiting impatiently our return. Even at that early age Stephen was something of a dictator, and we all have wryly amusing memories of the way, even from his pram, he would dominate our lives. Every afternoon we would carry the pram down the steps to the Cove, and then wheel it slowly along the front and up the hill to meet the children coming from school. On the way, very often we would like to have paused – but the moment we did so there were ominous rumbling moves from the old green pram, and a round shocked face would glare at us, prior to the emission of a horrible shrill wailing complaint. It was the same whoever might be wheeling the pram, and Gill and Jane would accept any other punishment rather than to have to wheel 'the Monster,' as he was (with a certain amount of affection) familiarly known.

The one we felt most sorry for was Martin, for with the arrival of another boy he had to give up the privilege of his own bedroom (only recently acquired) and share with Stephen. This was of course for our own convenience rather than Martin's. The general tendency being to want to get 'the Monster' to bed just as soon as possible, this meant that Martin was rather deprived of most of the pleasure of his own room. 'Be *very quiet* when you go up, Martin' … 'Don't put the light on, you might wake Stephen.' The prospect of Stephen awake was sufficiently alarming to ensure Martin's agreement …

However, I'm glad to say that brotherly love survived those early days, and their relationship has remained a happy one through twenty years of coming and going.

From this early age, then, Stephen showed a determined and even aggressive character. It was not so much that he was belligerent, though he could be on occasions, but more that he always expected his own way. Perhaps we were at fault in some way in not making some stand against this childhood autocrat, for I have a feeling we often gave way for the sake of peace. At any rate he managed to pass through childhood and even teenagehood into adulthood, and is still, as far as I can see, getting his own way.

Stephen's determination was no doubt one of the factors that helped to land him in a number of childhood scrapes. If anyone had the idea of raiding an orchard, or playing some practical joke, then we could be sure that Stephen was in the forefront. Perhaps his most famous escapade happened some years later, in St Ives, the occasion of the mass window breaking. At the time of the occurrence Stephen's alleged participation seemed to us, injured (and innocent) parents, laughable. When a police officer called inquiring about the breakage of 72 windows at a nearby warehouse we were indignant that he should even dare to suspect one of our children. However, we promised to ask them and received outraged denials from the others. From Stephen, however – and how our hearts sank! – we received no denial, merely a curious, slow rather wicked smile.

'*Seventy-two,* was it? Phew … ! Fancy that. I must tell Michael and Paul … '

But how – why – ? It turned out that Stephen and his friends had been playing a game called 'smash and grab.' Fortunately Stephen survived this extravaganza after we had all made a rather abject appearance before a local juvenile court.

Looking back it is difficult not to recognise that Stephen's childhood career consisted mainly of a long list of similarly dramatic events. Orchard-raiding, school-skiving, late night parties – you name it, Stephen organised it. His only saving grace was that he appeared to be the brainiest child of the family, and was usually able to charm his way out of situations for which there would otherwise have been no excuse.

Of all this, of course, there were only early premonitions in those summery days at Peter's Cottage, when Stephen's disruptive influence was comparatively confined to wilfully tipping over his pram, or crawling into some awkward corners of the house. Quite honestly, we were finding life more and more difficult ... particularly Jess, since she had just become pregnant again, and wasn't feeling at all well.

One afternoon she went into Penzance shopping, and decided to spend the night with her mother, who had recently moved to Penzance. At eight o'clock the next morning she had a severe haemorrhage and was rushed into Penzance hospital for immediate blood tranfusions. I knew nothing about this until about eleven when her sister rang me up, and I dashed into Penzance by car. When I got to the hospital Jess was very ill with blood transfusions still going on – she had at one stage been so bad that a priest (without being invited!) had said the last rites over her.

If she had had a miscarriage out at Sennen Cove she would undoubtedly have lost her life – only the fact that for no particular reason she had chosen to spend the night in Penzance and was close to the hospital there saved her life. This sort of thing makes one wonder. Once again, was it pure chance? I cannot be sure, but I do know that incidents of that sort, where life and death are acutely counter-played, make one see things in their proper perspective. I felt utterly lost and bereft, as did the children, and once we were all together again Jess and I felt for a long time a new undercurrent of closeness.

Soon after this we began to have frequent visits from our old friend, Lisa of Lelant, whose marriage had broken up leaving her with a three-year-old daughter, Pandora. One way and another she was delightful company and we always welcomed the sight of her bravely climbing the stone steps from the bus stop, carrying Pandora in her arms.

Indeed, after a while it began to seem to us all that this tiring journey could be avoided.

'Why don't you come and live with us?' said Jess, ever the practical one. 'I mean on a business-like basis. You can help look after the children, and in return we'll pay you and give you board and lodging, that sort of thing.'

'Yes,' I said, getting interested, as ever in any new venture.

'There's that tiny house outside, it'll be just right with a few improvements.'

Lisa was only too pleased to agree, and meanwhile we got a local builder in to work on what we vaguely called the out-house. This consisted of one downstairs room and two minute bedrooms. The main drawback was that the rear of the place was built against the steep walls of granite and consequently there was a general atmosphere of damp – and across the centre of the bottom room a decided trickle of water pursued its course along a worn groove in the cement. We had always assumed that when we came to do the place up it would be easy to get rid of this, but now in practice this proved quite impossible. During the whole of Lisa's tenancy, though she was quite happy in her tiny cottage she had to live with a perpetual stream running across her living room floor, though mostly covered up by straw mats.

It was one of the delightful things about Lisa that she always took such things in her stride. She always saw the funny side of an incident, however upsetting at the time. Both Jess and I warmed to her presence in the house, and the three of us got on very well, while the children and Pandora also seemed to take to one another.

It was, of course, because of the children, and especially our somewhat difficult younger son, that we had suggested Lisa joining us. The idea was that she should help look after Stephen during the day and do some baby-sitting at night. Lisa more than did her share of helping about the house: what we had not quite allowed for was the precipitate development of her own separate life in the locality.

Perhaps we made our first cardinal mistake, one evening when another friend was available to baby-sit, when we invited Lisa to come with us for drinks at the First and Last Pub. The result was a very gay evening, during which Lisa became quite the belle of the pub, an evening that ended with Jess and me returning a little uneasily, on our own, while Lisa was wafted off for a joy ride on a local boy's motor bike.

After that somehow we began to see less of Lisa in the evenings. It began innocently enough with her poking her head round the kitchen door one evening and calling out cheerfully, 'Just going for a stroll to the First and Last. Do you mind keeping an ear open for Pandy? I left her fast asleep.'

This was reasonable enough one or two evenings of the week. We did not even complain of the fact that, no matter how asleep Lisa thought her child was, invariably about half an hour after her departure Pandora would wander into our kitchen in her dressing gown saying she wanted a drink, or couldn't go to sleep. But gradually the whole process became speeded up and one day we suddenly woke up to the fact that Lisa had been out ten nights in a row, while we ourselves had stayed in baby-sitting for her for ten nights. At this we felt bound to stand up for our rights to get out just a little.

Lisa was sweetly apologetic and a new approach to the problem was essayed by her having her current boy friend come back to visit her several evenings, so that once again we were free to go out. As, frequently, we didn't particularly want to go out on specified evenings, the net result was that the four of us would join forces in a scrap meal and a talk round the fire.

Yes, they were happy, rather romantic days living at Land's End, forever associated in my mind with our first mutual bundle of trouble, the Monster in the green pram. Wherever we went now, it had to be taken. Most afternoons we would go out on to the marvellous wide white sand, and that meant lugging the old pram, and its content, over the rocks ... or sometimes we might fancy climbing up among the sand dunes and cliffs – no question of going on our own, the old pram had to come too!

Sometimes the whole family would drive in our old Rover (the Austin had expired and been replaced by an even older coupé which allowed for a large contingent) and visit Porthcurno Beach. Nowhere else in Cornwall is the water quite so clear, a ravishing greeny-blue of Mediterranean intensity. Sometimes we would spend whole stolen days of bliss, sunbathing and swimming and taking our picnic lunch. And often the more energetic ones would later climb the stone steps winding up to that strange phenomenon, a theatre on the cliffs.

I feel sorry for anyone who has never paid a summer visit to the Minack to watch the work of Shakespeare or Euripides or perhaps Fry or Ibsen or Shaw, played in that romantic setting. They have missed a unique experience. There cannot anywhere in the world be quite such a pleasure as to sit in the amphitheatre with the play outlined on the spotlit greensward below, while a vast backcloth of moonlit scenery stretches to the horizon, broken perhaps here and there by the flickering lights of the Newlyn fishing fleet steaming out to sea. Magic, pure magic.

Nanjizel, Porthgwarra, Porthcurno, Logan Rock, Penberth, Lamorna ... truly the Land's End dweller is surrounded by beautiful things. Of course, we were lucky in being able to take the romantic view. Down in Sennen Cove many of the old cottages were inhabited by families of fishing folk whose weather beaten faces and guarded expressions bore eloquent testimony to the hard lives they led. We were always very conscious of this barrier, of being strangers, and I think from the beginning we must have appreciated that our stay would not be a long one. But for two whole years we lived our lives steeped in that very strange, brooding atmosphere ... and I often wonder how much of it may have impregnated not only my own Scorpionic soul, but the equally Scorpionic character of our very Cornish son Stephen Roskelly.

V

Demelza

The auction was held in a big hall in the centre of Penzance. It wasn't by any means the first auction we had attended since settling in Cornwall. On and off during the past three years we must have attended a dozen or more, invariably as mere spectators, knowing our inability to make an effective bid, yet drawn like moths to the flame by the tantalising temptations.

But now at last we were to be active participants. In the space of a few hectic months we had managed to find a purchaser for Peter's Cottage and raised a prospective mortgage for our next home, and here we were to fight all kinds of unknown forces in a bid to purchase the former vicarage of the parish of St Hilary, some two miles beyond Marazion, a large rambling old house of seventeen rooms standing in three acres of overgrown land.

It all now depended on the auction. As we approached the hall on that fateful morning we felt like nervous wrecks. Our spirits weren't raised by seeing an enormous crowd of people gathered in the hall, even though we should have known from previous experience that in Cornwall attending auctions is for many people a form of light amusement, like going to the cinema, only cheaper. Supposing they had all come prepared to bid for the Old Vicarage? How could we compete, when we knew that on no account could we bid more than £2,000? Our hearts sank as we looked round at these potential competitors. With something like hatred we contemplated possible buyers who, without a qualm, would rob us of our one desire.

Our hearts sank further as we became aware that a number of good friends had come along, presumably to give moral support. During our years in Cornwall we had naturally gravitated to the bohemian world of painters and writers, potters and poets and woodchoppers. This was our world, indeed, and grateful we had been for their friendship. But today, just this one occasion when bank balances, sober appearance, civic responsibility and all other attributes of the more conventional world were the things that were bound to count …

There they sat, almost like a row of soldiers: four beards, one eccentric poet, a bald literary critic and two brazen hussies in tight-fitting jeans. We could not avoid them, we could not refuse their kindly well-meant greeting. They had saved two seats of honour among them in the very front row. Furtively we slunk down the corridor and into our places, conscious of the curious eyes of the auctioneer and several solicitors watching us.

But as the proceedings began and it became apparent there were several other houses to be disposed of first, and the tension eased, we too recovered our sense of proportion and began to be glad our friends had rallied round. For Jess, who gets wound up with inner tensions on such occasions it was difficult to relax, but I began to warm to my temporary spotlight.

At last the auctioneer, Thurstan Lane, cleared his throat and announced that he was putting up the Old Vicarage. What was he offered?

I waited nervously for someone to start the bidding. After a while finding silence more terrifying than a bid I stuttered:

'A thousand pounds.'

At this a pained smile passed over Thurstan Lane's face. However, to my astonishment he accepted the bid and asked for any advance.

Now our hearts, which had begun to lighten, felt weighed down with despair, as from another part of the hall a strong Cornish accent said:

'One thousand and two hundred and fifty pounds.'

I looked at Jess. This was it. The battle was on. Around me I felt the beards wagging and my friends egging me on with their kindly thoughts.

'One thousand three hundred pounds.'

Slowly, inexorably the bidding went on.

'One thousand five hundred pounds,' I said, marvelling at the steady note in my voice.

'One thousand six hundred pounds,' returned the Cornish voice defiantly.

'One thousand seven hundred pounds,' I said firmly.

'One thousand seven hundred and fifty,' spoke up the now more cautious rival bidder.

We began to creep along in fifties and twenty-fives. Now and then the bidding hung fire altogether and Thurstan Lane, in his jovial manner, tried to liven things up.

It was at one of these stages that our friend Arthur Caddick, the poet, stirring from his reverie, stood up, his gaunt frame swaying slightly, and asked in his booming voice:

'Sir, is it true there are two curates locked up in the hall cupboard, and if so do they go with the Vicarage?'

There was a stir and a ripple of laughter, but, I fanced, a slightly uneasy ripple, as if most of the people could not allow their ingrown suspicions of the bohemian world to be overridden by the sheer humour of the remark. It was then, I think, that I suddenly began to feel that we were going to get the Old Vicarage. It was such a white elephant, such an extraordinary hotch-potch both to look at and in its history. It was a place already famous for having been a home of a succession of rather eccentric priests, including Bernard Walke, famous for his Nativity Plays broadcast by the BBC, and Sandys Wason, leaving the neighbouring parish of Cury-by-Gunwalloe and arriving at St Hilary with all his belongings piled into a furniture van. During Walke's incumbency many famous artists and writers had dined with him at the Vicarage, among them Compton Mackenzie, Bernard Shaw and Alfred Munnings. Now that the Vicarage was to become worldly, signified (by legal agreement) by the prefix 'old,' it seemed only right it should be inhabited and visited by writers and artists and other rebels against the orderly imprisoning routines of life.

'Two thousand pounds,' I said nervously.

It seemed to me an awesome few moments of silence. Jess and I both went hot and cold all over, hardly daring to look at one another. Besides us we felt the tension spread right along our row of friends: even the beards quivered with fearful anticipation. Then somehow the atmosphere changed.

Suddenly I became aware that the silence was continuing, that there had been *no answering bid.*

With an air of impending finality Thurstan Lane picked up his little mallet and brandished it in the air.

'For the last time ladies and gentlemen. Two thousand pounds is the bid. Going for two thousand pounds – once!' Crash went the mallet. 'Twice!' Another crash. 'Going for the third and last time – '

The mallet fell decisively on the table and almost in the same gesture Thurstan Lane waved in my direction.

'Sold to the gentleman over there for two thousand pounds.' He put down the hammer and nodded: and then, so I am reliably informed, muttered discreetly: 'And God help the Old Vicarage.'

*

Almost the first thing we did after moving into the Old Vicarage was to increase its population. Although she had helped manfully in the early work of getting the Vicarage ready for habitation, Jess was in fact within a few weeks of having our second baby – which somehow we took for granted, by the law of averages, would be a girl. Somewhere about this time I had come across the books of Winston Graham, a popular author well known for his thrillers, many of which have been filmed, like *Marnie,* and for his series of fascinating novels about family life in Cornwall during the eighteenth century – the *Poldark* novels as they are known. Later on we were to have the pleasure of meeting Winston Graham, who then lived at Perranporth on the North Coast of Cornwall, but at this time I had no reason for reading the *Poldark* books other than their sheer fascination of detail and characterisation. Particularly Demelza, the warm-hearted, impulsive mischievious, wayward and wholly delightful heroine ... She seemed to me every man's ideal.

'If it's a girl, let's call her Demelza.'

'What a beautiful name,' said Jess. 'What does it mean?'

'It's a Cornish word. It means "Thy Sweetness." '

So Demelza she was called when she first opened her eyes to

the world in that gracious bedroom with the magnolia tree writhing its way up the side and filling one of the windows with its soft blossom. Demelza Ann Val Baker, neat and plump, and as dark as her brother Stephen, now romping round with a three-year old's curiosity, was fair.

From the beginning the Old Vicarage was very much a children's house, and this was as it should be. For too long the house had stood empty, although in years gone by, we gathered, it had reverberated to the sound of childish laughter from a succession of large families. Indeed one of the previous vicars had been responsible for the addition of the curious squat tower that had been erected at the very top of the Vicarage – an escape room to which he could flee from the rampaging of his brood. Sometimes I, too, cast an envious eye on that room, but I was for ever put off attempting to settle there by the revelation that it was quite possibly haunted by the spirit of some unfortunate young man who had jumped to death out of the big bay window.

In fact this window – which looked out over the fields and down to St Michael's Mount rising out of the sea in the distance – was the only window that really had an impressive view. For the rest, the windows of the Old Vicarage tended to look inwards, to the more immediate reality of our life in its three acres, enclosed either by moss-covered walls or rows of old trees.

And what a friendly old home it was to be! Not only was the Vicarage old, it was definitely odd. It rambled all over the place with rooms jutting out here, there and everywhere, and little flights of steps darting unexpectedly up, so that almost every room seemed to be on a different level. The kitchen was in quite a different part of the house from the sitting room. The bathroom was over the coal cellar – and of course miles from any of the bedrooms. Although nearly all the rooms were on two floors, there were still two higher floors to the house, the top one devoted entirely to the long room I have mentioned, and above that yet another loft. These later floors, it appeared, had been added on as a Victorian afterthought to a Georgian type of building – the result being most offensive, aesthetically. Viewed from the lane the Vicarage looked rather

like a huge aircraft carrier whose super-structure reared up out
of all proportion to the rest.

For the children it was something of a paradise. Quite apart
from the spaciousness of the house with its seventeen rooms,
they could disappear for hours down among the undergrowth,
following in single file between the trees, playing cowboys and
Indians. There were outhouses abounding, some of them full
of old bedsteads and lumps of coal. There was a derelict walled
orchard next door which offered tremendous temptations
(seldom resisted, I regret to report). And in the house itself
there were seemingly endless corridors, leading to room after
room. No wonder, under such circumstances, the children
seemed to blossom out and assert themselves as individual
units in the family.

And none more strikingly than this very youngest blob of
humanity, Demelza. Naturally, we could not as yet read into
her future, see her dark and elfin-like, a sensitive and rather
nervous child with a vivid imagination showing, along with an
elemental and romantic nature, a shy gentleness, also a
surprising tomboy attraction, symbolised by her wearing a Red
Indian hat and brandishing a tomahawk and yelling out blood-
thirsty threats. We did not yet know of the surprising religious
streak in her nature which, coupled with great excitability was
to lead to her running into our bedroom, eyes shining
brightly, crying out: 'I've just been to *Holy Commotion*.'

We had early foretastes of that instinct for the drama which
we had learned from Jane, is a strong characteristic of the child
born under Virgo ('Oh, God, another Virgo, all those scenes!')
… But we had not yet experienced all the drama within drama
of Demelza going to the Italia Conti Drama School in London
and then chucking it all up through the inability to concentrate
– later to some extent redeeming herself by the considerable
initiative of joining the exclusive London buskers' brigade
and, as a bottler, sometimes earning the fabulous sums of £25
in a single evening. Ah, happy days …

No, for now Demelza was still a tiny black-haired thing,
plump and contented, and seemingly all that a pretty young
baby daughter should be. Owing to the liberal geography of
the Old Vicarage we had been able to scatter the children

around with a room of their own each, and Demelza was no exception being given a small, but secluded, room looking over the back garden. This would have been fine if it were not for the fact that she turned out to be a somewhat troubled sleeper. Indeed, this was the beginning of a lifelong nervousness of the dark ... We found that there were only two sure ways to encourage Demelza to a relatively comfortable night's sleep. One was to leave a lighted night-light by her bedside ... and the other, unfortunately for me, was for someone to rush in and briefly soothe her alarm when, as regularly as clockwork, she woke up with a cry at precisely one o'clock every night.

Why one o'clock I shall never know, but it is a time that became engraved in my consciousness in those early months of Demelza's first years on earth. For Jess, probably like most wives, felt that she had done her share, what with the day's washing of nappies, feeding, bathing and so on. And so every night when that dreaded and rather piercing cry began to waft through the house, there was a meaningful dig in my side, and the significant comment: 'She's *your* daughter.'

Of this there could be no dispute (and indeed Demelza of all the children is the spitting image of my own mother, from whom she must have derived so many of those fears and apprehensions) and there was nothing for it but to bestir myself, and pad through the long corridors. It was in fact quite a long journey, out of our room, down one landing, up another, through Martin's room and past Stephen's, and finally into the tiny room which by now reverberated with rhythmical piercing cries. After a while I could have made the journey blindfold, and might as well have done for I did not like to put on any light for fear of waking any of the other children. I learned speed, too, for the sooner I arrived at my destination, the sooner there might be an end to the fearful racket.

I brought it to an end, of course, in the time-honoured manner of all fathers in the middle of the dark lonely night by picking up the warm cuddly bundle of humanity and cosseting her into a close soothing embrace, rocking her slightly and murmuring sweet nothings. How often down the long years of ups and downs, of pleasures and disappointments, of hopes and frustrations, have I remembered, rather wistfully, those shadowy moments when the universe and I stood still, there in the middle of a summer's night with the sweet smell of magnolias wafting through the tiny window, lulling my troubled first daughter off into dreamland.

*

After a while at St Hilary we were able to get Stephen into the infants section of the local village school. Every morning (much to our relief), Martin, Gill, Jane and now Stephen, all set off down the winding country lane to the school, and Jess and I were left in comparative peace, with only the green pram and its newest occupant. We were reminded often of our early days at Peter's Cottage, where we had enjoyed this daytime peace in the same way, with Stephen ... but there were subtle changes. Gone were the booming sea, the rearing cliffs, the eternal whining winds ... now the pram stood in the sheltered back garden, near the dark green leaves of the rhododendron trees, alive with the hum of bees and the smell of magnolias, all very peaceful ... And somehow as a baby, too, Demelza was the opposite of Stephen. Whereas the male animal had been a tough and rather troublesome one, the female, it seemed was placid and peaceful. Certainly Demelza was the least trouble of all our babies – paradoxically, that, since there can be little doubt that she became the most temperamental, exasperating and exhausting of our teenagers.

I can remember an incident, later on in our family life, which perfectly illustrates this change in Demelza. This was soon after a time when Stephen had been given glasses to wear, and was somewhat dolefully going off to school every morning wearing a pair of rather grim National Health spectacles (he had little choice, poor lad, as he had developed chronic short sightedness). We were puzzled a day or two later, to find Demelza groping her way about the kitchen, a look of dramatic horror on her face.

'It's no good – I can't see – where are you – I can't see – '

At first we were alarmed, but then it soon became apparent that Demelza was exaggerating considerably, or so it seemed.

Certainly when she wanted to, she seemed able to see.

But she persisted, and demanded to be taken to see the eye specialist in Penzance. Dr Rostrom examined her in detail and could find nothing wrong. Such a specialist's verdict meant nothing to Demelza.

'I tell you I can't see. I need glasses.'

After two instances of her being found in the main street holding her hands ahead of her and acting as if she was completely blind, and being brought home by a sympathetic policeman, we took her along again to see Dr Rostrom. Fortunately he was a wise man, and after Demelza emerged beaming triumphantly, he beckoned us in.

'Your daughter is suffering from a rather specialised complaint,' he said with a twinkle. 'You might call it hysterical blindness.'

'She's not – ?'

'No, no, there's nothing wrong with her eyes at all. However she has convinced herself there is – so I have prescribed her a pair of glasses. Plain lenses of course, but I think that should do the trick.'

It did too. For a week Demelza wore her glasses – sought out of jealousy of Stephen having something she didn't – and then she quickly lost interest. Years later I found them on a junk heap of old things.

Yes, there was never a dull moment while Demelza Ann Val Baker was around.

VI

Genevieve

Our early years at the Old Vicarage were haunted, perhaps dominated is a more exact word, by money, or rather the lack of money. As a free-lance writer I had long ago grown accustomed to the haphazard financial aspects of such a life, but of course it is a very different thing being a free-lance writer who only has to keep himself, or perhaps a wife and say one child even – and being a very apprehensive father with a large family to feed and clothe and keep. Unfortunately my earlier financial success as an author had not continued its hopeful upward trend, and instead my earning capacity seemed to have levelled out at around £1,000 a year. Worse still, this income, such as it was, came in the most sporadic bursts, so that one week I might get a cheque for £50, or even £100 – but for the next month, nothing at all.

Altogether we found ourselves going through a very hazardous time. Saturday mornings – rent day in those good old days – were now approached not with hope but with fear, for we knew we had to have at least two pounds to see the family through the week-end. Sometimes one of my own payments would come through and the situation would be saved, but only too often the post contained no more than bills and returned manuscripts. Then indeed my writer's imagination had to work fast. If there was no money in the bank and our friends were in much the same state of financial depression there was only one possible course left, and that was to sell something.

In London and other large centres there exist pawnshops to cater for just such emergencies – in Cornwall, alas, there are no pawnshops as such. The best we could find in Penzance was a tiny shop near the Post Office where whole suits could be bought for ridiculous sums like seven shillings, or a second hand shop in Chapel Street where old Mr White might give a few shillings for twenty-four gramophone records, or a heap of old books. Later I found another gift shop which provided a curious and unexpected market for odd pieces of pottery and ornaments, and old copies of the *Cornish Review*.

Looking back, a picture of a typical Saturday morning of this period can be seen as a tragic-comic epic. First we would embark on a frantic search around the Old Vicarage for anything sellable (children excluded, sometimes rather grudgingly). If it was a real emergency then I, personally, would be quite ruthless – treasured books, old pictures, family heirlooms, all would go by the board. In this way I not only disposed of many excellent novels belonging to me by Graham Greene, Henry Miller, Aldous Huxley, Evelyn Waugh, etc., but also accidentally a few of Jess's books (a mishap for which I have never been quite forgiven). Having found enough articles we would then stuff them all into the back of the current car – by this time we had 'progressed' from the Rover to an old London taxi, bought for £50 from the taxi company's garage at Brixton. I believe ours was one of only two London taxis in Cornwall in those days (the other belonged to Mary John, wife of Augustus John's son Caspar, over at Mousehole), and I suppose we must have made quite a striking sight, piled high with various articles plus all the children, all hungry and hopeful for their pocket money.

At last, with a honk on the old fashioned bulb horn, we would circle the Old Vicarage drive and set off on the vital journey ... At least we would if there was enough petrol to get us to Penzance. Often there wasn't, and this meant borrowing half a crown for half a gallon from our friend Donald Swan, in the studio near by. If there was no money and no petrol we had one last grim choice *in extremis* the family would have to get out and literally push the old taxi about a quarter of a mile along the drive and down the road through Goldsithney to a point where it was just possible to free-wheel as far as Marazion, where there was a garage which would supply us with petrol on credit.

On arrival at Penzance, we would have to start the nerve-racking round of the hock shops, a case of the family waiting with fingers crossed while I furtively staggered in carrying my load of books, records and so forth. Sometimes I might emerge beaming with a handful of notes, but often I would come out with a hang-dog look, perhaps still carrying a pile of rejected goods, and the whole business would have to be tried again at another shop. Somehow, thank goodness, we always seemed to manage to raise enough money at least to buy the basic week-end food, give the children their pocket money and five bob to get some fish and chips, and a few shillings over to enable us to retire to meet our friends for a mid-day drink at the old St John's House.

By the time we had settled the children with their fish and chips in the roomy back of the taxi, in the car park, and reached our own haven we were often emotionally exhausted, and I suppose this showed. I shall never forget one morning when we went in and said mournfully, 'It'll have to be half a bitter each today.' A quiet lady in a tweed coat who had been sitting in the corner suddenly beckoned Jess over and asked if she could have a word with her outside. When she got Jess out she said: 'I often see you in here and admire your good spirits. I don't like to see you in difficulties. Would you mind accepting this?' – and into my wife's hand she pressed a pound note. A spontaneous, very sweet gesture, much appreciated.

I find it difficult to convey the full sense of what it means to live in this fashion, always balanced on a tight-rope above disaster – a life of very great strain. Not the sort of life obviously which is helped by the responsibility for a large family ... which made it pretty understandable how Jess felt when she discovered that once more we might expect an addition to that family. What made it all the more daunting was that we had taken every possible precaution not to have any more children – we had more than enough! Jess was furious and upset, the whole blame was attached to me, and life became miserable – made more miserable, of course, by the fact that Jess was always very ill during the early months of pregnancy. More than once she did all she knew to get rid of the unwanted baby, but I guess when they are intended to arrive on earth, they determindedly do just that.

The circumstances of our last child's birth are very clearly etched in my own mind. Ironically enough, for about a year beforehand we had temporarily let a couple of rooms at the Old Vicarage to the local mid-wife, Nurse Ford, while she waited for builders to complete work on a house she had bought nearby. Now, when we could have done with her on the spot, she had moved out of the Vicarage and into her own home. Fortunately it was not too far away, and when at two in the morning Jess appeared to have gone into labour I drove hastily round to fetch the Nurse, on what proved to be a false alarm – indeed, Jess was having what is known in the trade as a false birth.

Naturally, I felt rather guilty about disturbing the sleep of an elderly lady due to retire shortly. When, three weeks later labour appeared to start again, I was quite hesitant about calling the Nurse – especially as once again (it always is!) it was the middle of the night. However, in the end I went and fetched her – just as well, as she had hardly reached our bedroom before Genevieve, true to her placid and equable character, arrived quickly and neatly and with the minimum of fuss.

After hearing that inevitable strange cry which signified yet another V.B. loose in the world I hurriedly made a pot of tea and arrived back in the bedroom bearing this welcome refreshment – almost at the very moment when Nurse Ford, probably tired after her night's work, slipped over and fell with a resounding thud full length on the floor, taking the afterbirth with her, a horrible mess. What's more she found herself quite unable to get up again, having obviously sprained her leg quite severely. Very thankful that it hadn't happened ten minutes earlier, when I should have had to deliver Genevieve myself, I had first to complete the general tidying up process under the nurse's directions, then carry her to her car and drive her home, where she had to stay in bed for several weeks.

From the beginning Genevieve Dilys Val Baker tended to be the sugar plum fairy of the family. After all (we were somehow grimly determined) she was definitely the last of the brood! As is well known the youngest is always the spoiled one, and perhaps Genevieve, lying there all golden and rather beautiful, already sensed this built in advantage. As she grew older she was to develop a grave rather Alice-in-Wonderland beauty – she even had the conventional long golden locks. There was indeed something rather story-bookish about her presence, and of course Jess and I immediately forgot all about our arguments and objections, and doted on this wonderful new baby. Even the other children appeared to approve, and it wasn't until thirteen years later, when she became a rather advanced teenager, nudging into their lives, that the other children really began to find any real objections!

Soon after Genevieve placidly entered our lives Demelza became old enough to join the other children at school, and so once again Jess and I had our old familiar experience of being alone during the daytime with the one tiny infant. I am inclined to think that this routine worked out to advantage, for it meant that each of our children had a private year with his or her parent, a chance to get to know each other. So once again there were summery days where a little naked girl lay in the sun on the lawn at St Hilary while Jess and I busied ourselves with one or other of our various schemes for augmenting our income … I think this must have been about the time of 'Jess's violets.'

'We must think big – plant them on a big scale. We'll make a fortune!'

This I hasten to explain was Jess speaking, not me. She brimmed over with confidence and vitality about the prospects … who was I to voice a vague half-intuitive idea that no good would come of it all?

'Mind you,' said Jess warningly. 'It's essential to keep the ground hoed. Violets must have *plenty* of air and space.'

But of course yes, we agreed. We would hoe them most diligently. And so we would have done – if it had not been for the bees. They were not our bees, dear me, no. If they had been we might have been able to do something about them. They were bees belonging to the gentlemen who had rented the next-door walled fruit garden. Day after day great swarms of bees abruptly deserted the humdrum existence of their fruit garden to explore the more interesting world of our garden.

Later we were told that the real cause of the trouble may have been the introduction of the wrong strain of Italian Queens into the hives, thoroughly upsetting the entire family.

Anyway the cause didn't matter, what was so disastrous was the result. This was quite simply, that every time Jess or I or any grown up appeared in the back garden he or she was immediately attacked by a vicious swarm of angry bees. It became quite commonplace for me to hear a blood-curdling scream and look up to see an agitated human figure dancing a jig in the garden. The bees were quite relentless: it was impossible even to venture twenty feet into the garden without their zooming up from nowhere and launching their attack.

Only the children escaped – a mystery for a long time until Jess worked out that the line of the bees flight was about four feet from ground level so they passed over the children's heads. In the end a Ministry of Agriculture Adviser arrived at our urgent summons and finally had the hives removed and we were able at last to venture into the garden in peace. But by then, alas, the violets had vanished forever into a jungle of weeds, all two thousand of them.

That was Jess's scheme. My own was equally doomed, I suppose. One day a strange little man, Mr W. came out to the Old Vicarage, and after a lot of beating around the bush put up an odd proposition. He had noticed he said, that we had a lot of dead trees around, as well as many standing that could no doubt be cut down. Well, he could guarantee a regular sale for fire-wood logs – supposing he and I went into partnership? He would cut the logs up, and I would provide the transport and help to deliver them to houses from where he had got orders – we would split the money fifty-fifty.

By now I was so desperate about money that I was ready to grasp any straw in the wind. Every day little Mr W. came out with a saw and worked away cutting up logs. From somewhere we procured a lot of old potato sacks and the children enthusiastically filled up them with logs. After two or three days of this we loaded the taxi up and set off. People often used to say, didn't you feel rather humiliated? I don't think so, because both with the hocking of old books and now the selling of logs I always saw these things as adventures.

Mind you, I was a bit taken aback, after we drove slowly up and down one or two quiet back streets of Penzance, to realise that Mr W. had been exaggerating when he implied he had orders waiting. What he was now doing was hawking the wood from door to door, hoping to sell it on the spot. In fact, logs being in demand, we usually did manage to get rid of our load. After I had paid for the petrol, calculated the hours of my time wasted, apart from the physical fatigue of carrying heavy sacks up and down garden paths it began to seem to me that the 10s.0d. (50p) or so I was left with after a day was hardly worth the candle. However we carried on until one day, in pouring rain, I staggered up to a back door to deliver a couple of sacks – and found myself being paid by my assistant bank manager. Somehow this seemed to put things into perspective, and I decided I had better get on with some more writing.

Genevieve became associated more directly with my writing than the other children. At the Old Vicarage I had a rather pleasant large study looking over the back garden, and for many months it became the custom for Genevieve to be put on the floor and left to play with her toys ... while I kept an eye on her. At first she was in a play-pen, but later we dispensed with that, and instead she had the freedom of the study. She was, of course, fascinated by my typing, and would spend hours gravely watching my finger movements. Having been trained as a newspaper reporter I have always been able to write under pretty well any conditions, and so now I was not at all put out by my new companion. Indeed, I rather enjoyed being able to turn every now and then and conduct imaginary conversations with this little mite who could, of course, barely utter more than a 'Goooo!'

Perhaps these early experiences had a more profound effect on Genevieve than I realised at the time. Alone among the family, really, she has shown distinct interest in writing. Many years later, she was always to be found lying on her bed with a writing pad in front of her composing long and intricate stories and poems. In her early teens she went to the School of St Clare's at Penzance, and there she was a regular contributor to the school magazine. Genevieve also revealed quite a talent for drawing, one which in later years Jess made use of in her pottery, encouraging Genny to decorate large plates. Paradoxically enough Genevieve's very prettiness and normality may partially count against her progress as a writer or painter. Almost everyone who meets her immediately sees her as an obvious candidate for an early marriage and motherhood – she is very good with children. And yet perhaps under all that there lurks a talented artist waiting to get out – who knows?

*

It was during Genevieve's early months that, having taken a course of pottery at Penzance Art School under Michael Leach, Jess decided to start her own pottery at St Hilary. We scraped together £15 to buy an old kick wheel, ordered a couple of hundredweight of clay and a small electric kiln – and we were in business. Soon I was off on the road in our old taxi calling round gift shops and rather to everyone's surprise, actually getting orders. Thus was born a business which, like my writing, remained with us (thank goodness!) down the years.

But of course, in order to operate a pottery Jess simply had to have some assistance, and here began the saga of our *Helps*. Someone told us that the best place to advertise was in *The Lady,* and that if we were prepared to take someone with a small child of her own we should have no difficulties. Well ... we advertised and someone wrote and in due course I had a wire to meet her at Penzance station. No doubt the peremptory nature of the telegram should have given us some fleeting glimpse of what was to come, but it didn't. Dutifully I put aside my morning's work and drove the six miles into town to meet the train. At the station I scanned the passengers getting off the train and was just concluding that our help had missed the train when I became aware of an elegantly dressed young woman standing by the door of a first class compartment, in her arms a small infant curled up in a beautiful Paisley shawl.

Upon approaching and making inquiry I was given a gracious smile and acknowledgement and directed to the luggage van. There in a row stood a mammoth luxury pram, four suitcases, a trunk and several other articles. While the new help stood by I laboriously carried her possessions out of the station and loaded them into the car. When all were squeezed in Queenie and her baby got delicately into the front seat and were driven to their new home.

While, perspiring somewhat, I unloaded all the luggage and carried it upstairs the elegant young lady made herself comfortable on our sofa, still nursing her infant.

'Isn't she sweet?' she said.

'Delightful,' said Jess. 'Er, we have some children, you'll be able to –'

'I wonder if you have some milk? Baby would like some milk.' Jess went into the kitchen and heated up some milk. When she brought it back Queenie took it with a smile and proceeded to feed her baby. While she was doing this Jess decided she had better get on with making lunch. When this was ready our new resident tucked her baby away in the pram, and sat down and ate a hearty meal.

After lunch we sat back expectantly.

Queenie rose and looked around.

'Would you mind if I took baby for a walk? She does like her afternoon parade.'

We looked at one another and said nothing. Queenie went for her walk, Jess sat and looked at the dirty plates for a long time, then carried them off to the kitchen.

When the baby came back from its walk tea time had arrived. Jess had made quite a nice tea, scones and strawberry jam. I think Queenie enjoyed it. Afterwards she put baby to bed, an operation which seemed to take rather a long time; by the time she emerged Jess had fed our children and put two of them to bed. Gill and Jane, who were still up, sat and stared at Queenie in awe: but Queenie seemed to take little notice of them. She announced, instead, her intention of unpacking – and this little job occupied her for the rest of the evening.

Ah, well, we thought it must be strange for her, she needs time to get settled in. But the next day was exactly the same: Jess ran round making meals for Queenie and on two occasions was called in to help her move her huge trunk. If you ask why we didn't speak to Queenie about the realities of her position and purpose I can only meekly reply that there was 'something about her.' Her pram, her clothes, her accessories, her baby and herself – all belonged to the lap of luxury. Everything she had was obviously of the best, spotlessly clean – by comparison our own clothes and things seemed incredibly shabby. It became increasingly obvious that one just couldn't ask such an aristocratic being to wash dishes or sweep floors.

We stood it for several days until Jess and I were hardly on speaking terms, and then, miraculously, Queenie herself put us out of our misery. She came to us one morning and explained quite sweetly that she was afraid the position didn't suit her. The children were rather noisy and kept baby awake, and the air was not to her taste. Later that day I loaded her things into the car and drove her back to the station. In the evening we felt happy for the first time for nearly a week.

A joke? Not at all. That was merely the first of many dramas. Our next experience was with an apparently hard-working type called Kathleen whose brief stay was interrupted by the arrival of two huge policemen, come to arrest her for having absconded from her last place of employment with a collection of jewellery, plates, blankets, clothes, money … The police had a complete list. They found everything in Kathleen's room.

We felt sorry for Kathleen but it was out of our hands.

'Well,' said Jess with a shrug, 'I suppose it's as well it came out now, before anything happened.'

Alas, I discovered, things *had* happened. Missing were possessions of our own, gone into the limbo with Kathleen. But we were too disheartened to do anything about it.

After this we laid down a new rule.

'No children. Definitely unmarried, unmotherly type only.'

That was how we came to have Frances. When I come to try to describe Frances, words almost fail me. 'Daughter of Darkness' was someone's phrase, and it about summed her up. She was only sixteen, but there was something about her that made you aware she was centuries old in cunning and secret experience. Sly, I suppose, was the adjective. She didn't walk, she seemed to sidle. She appeared and disappeared without making a sound. She had a high-pitched giggle that made me jump every time I heard it.

Looking back it seems incredible we ever engaged her, and yet at the time I remember we thought, well, she seems

reasonably bright and fond of children, and perhaps a young
person could be moulded into our way of life. Moulding
Frances took years off both our lives in fact, even though she
was with us a mere four months.

It wasn't so much anything she did or didn't do, so much as
her ways and mannerisms. At breakfast in the morning I would
be reading my paper and suddenly behind me would come that
weird cackle.

'What is it, Frances? What on earth's the matter?'

Frances would point at some minor headline in the paper.

'See that about the fellow cutting his wife's head off with a
hatchet? Coo!'

Morbid things fascinated Frances. She had an unerring eye
for the headline about the bus crash into a ravine, the
mysterious stranger striking again, the wife poisoner, and so
on. For a long time we were rather puzzled at Frances's
penchant for reading headlines until it emerged that she
couldn't really read anything beyond block letters.

Illiteracy was no real handicap for Frances, however. There
was more melodrama and fantasy in her small blonde head
than in almost any other head I can think of. If she walked
down to the village and back she was nearly raped three times
and definitely assaulted by the poor innocent postman. Men
indeed were something of an obsession with her. Baker,
grocer, electrician – all who entered Frances's domain in the
kitchen were subjected to the curious mixture of leers, winks
and smiles which composed her cinema-influenced technique
of flirtation.

Not surprisingly, Frances collected admirers. Gradually it
began to dawn on me in a dim sort of way that there was a
dangerously thin dividing line between her fantasies about
what happened on her outings – and hard facts. Nevertheless, I
told myself sternly, that was none of my business.

Then one day for no accountable reason Frances fixed her
lascivious eye upon me. One day she knocked on the study
door, entered, posed very dramatically – and her skirt fell
down. She took to leaning heavily upon my shoulder when
serving a meal and sometimes, furtively, under the table I
would feel a leg pressing suggestively against my own.

Even so, so anxious were we not to add to our chain of misfortune about helps, we might have carried on with Frances – had we not made the unexpected discovery that when we went out for an evening, leaving our children safely in her care as we imagined, Frances was catching the next bus into town after us, to meet one of her numerous boyfriends.

This had to be the end – the daughter of darkness had to go. For a time we tried to manage without anyone, and then, regretfully, we advertised again. This time there arrived in our midst – Florrie.

Like Frances, Florrie was a country girl. But Florrie wasn't sixteen and was no daughter of darkness. She was about thirty and plump in the grand tradition, sixteen stone at least – and like all plump people, jolly and cheerful. We watched affectionately as she settled comfortably into her new life. The children adored her, and she adored them. True she was very slow about the house, but she did eventually get through the work, and she was honest and well-meaning and cheerful. Good old Florrie!

Alas, fate was never on our side. Down the other end of our lane lived an elderly widower called Ben. Whiskery, red-nosed, comfort-loving, we did not hold a high opinion of his qualities. No matter – he cast a covetous eye upon Florrie, and it was too much. Florrie had never been wooed – but secretly it was her longing to be married, like all her friends. This, for his own reasons of wanting to be well fed and looked after, Ben was willing to offer. Soon the inevitable happened, Florrie gave notice and we were guests at her wedding in the little Methodist chapel at Goldsithney.

Just when we were in despair our old friend the *New Statesman* unwittingly came to our rescue. I saw there one day the constant advertisement which offers foreign girls *au pair,* and so wrote off for details. Back came a fascinating collection, rather like stud pedigrees, together with photographs of several very attractive French, Spanish and Italian girls.

At that time our friend Anthony Richards, who with his pottery partner Len was a constant visitor to the Old Vicarage, was very much a lone wolf, his marriage having ended. We used to show him photographs of the girls and say teasingly,

'Never mind, we're going to find you a lovely French girl.'
Anthony would grunt morosely, being in a state of cynicism
about women, but he approved, as we did, the details and
photograph of one, Christianne Cherrain, and after exchanging letters we decided to invite her over.

From the moment I met her off the train at Penzance I knew
that Christianne was just right for us. She was dark and pretty
and vivacious, and both Jess and I and the children love having
attractive people around us. Then too, she was so sweet
natured and had such a sense of humour – why, she even spoke
good English! – Oh, yes, she was going to be all right.

Somehow Christianne fitted exactly into the happy-go-lucky
atmosphere of the Old Vicarage. Indeed – alas, from the point
of view of her rather stern father who had expressly asked for a
post in Cornwall so as to be far away from the sinful
temptations of London, that wicked city! – she fell with the
greatest of ease into the vagaries of bohemian life. As the
daughter of a somewhat prim and fussily correct Frenchman
and a much more extrovert and half-Egyptian mother
Christianne was probably bound to have a streak of abandon
in her vivacious person. All the same, when we suddenly
received news that her father was arriving to pay a visit I don't
think we could possibly have imagined a more unfortunate
first impression. We had driven specially to Penzance station to
meet Monsieur Cherrain only to find there had been a mix up
and he had arrived an hour earlier and caught a taxi out to the
Old Vicarage. There he walked into the kitchen to find his
meek little daughter Christianne, sitting on the edge of the
kitchen table – posing for a portrait by our friend Donald
Swan.

It took us several days of excessive cordiality to thaw Mr
Cherrain out of his displeasure; but I must say that by the time
his visit was over we were all the greatest of friends. This
achievement was not without some cost, both financial and
psychological, for it was his custom to drink two bottles of
wine a day, and desperately we kept pace. But on the last
evening we sat around a roaring fire and were rather touched
when Monsieur Cherrain suddenly sang a little song, and
explained it was the customary procedure in France when you

wished to express how much you have enjoyed your stay.

So Christianne stayed on, helping especially to look after our very tiny, angelic Genevieve – the bond between them I think has lived on even into these days when Christianne has several of her own children ... who belong, by the way, to none other than our old friend Anthony! So we really did find him a bride!

Part Two

Beside the Seaside

I

The House on the Beach

Our family life began its unconventional career in a flat off
Fulham Road and continued through a variety of somewhat
eccentric bases: a converted cowshed on Trencrom Hill, a
glorified boarding house in Penzance, Peter's Cottage on the
edge of cliffs near Land's End, Bernard Walke's old vicarage at
St Hilary – and then, during a brief exile, the village of
Mersham, near Folkestone in Kent, and finally (full circle) a
house in Drayton Gardens, off the South Kensington end of
Fulham Road. We had moved out of Cornwall because of a
vague feeling that perhaps I would find more writing jobs
nearer the Metropolis, but in fact all that happened was that we
filled with an enormous nostalgia for our old home area.
Inevitably this nostalgia grew and grew, until at last we took
the step that perhaps we had always known we were going to
take: sold the lease of the London house and moved back
westwards – this time to St Ives itself.

From the moment we drove down the long slope into St Ives
and saw again that wonderful vista, the tiny dolls' houses
clustering around the harbour with the green hump of the
island behind, and the blue sweep of the sea beyond I think we
felt very conscious that, as a family, we had come to our
journey's end. In all our movements about Cornwall it had
always been to St Ives that we had come back repeatedly. Now
there was an enormous relief to be back, to be able to give way
at long last to a sense of belonging somewhere. But, of course,
two adults and six children can't just walk into a permanent
home like that – least of all in St Ives, where property is scarcer
and prices higher than almost anywhere else in Cornwall.

To give us a base to work from, I had taken a furnished

cottage with the somewhat romantic address, Virgin Street, and though the winter rent was cheap enough the conditions were appallingly cramped for a large family: the entire area of the cottage would not have taken more than half our drawing room at St Hilary. As it was, we were all sharing bedrooms, and eating and sitting in one small living-room, so that the winter was something of a strain.

In the middle of one night I awoke to hear Demelza screaming and after shouting to her several times to go to sleep I got out of bed to find the house full of smoke – thick, billowing, choking smoke. When I opened the door to try to go downstairs I had to shut it again to keep out a blast of hot air and flames. The house was on fire – and it had no rear windows or entrances at all. I called the children down into the front bedroom, and then clambered out of the window and managed to drop down to the street outside, at the same time yelling out 'Fire! Fire!' Soon the people around us were astir, and while with another man I opened the front door and went in and threw buckets of water on the flames in the living-room (clothes drying over a fire had dropped down and caught alight) Jess handed the children out of the window one by one, to be rushed off and wrapped up and given cups of tea by kindly neighbours. In the end the fire-brigade came, and we extinguished the flames: but had it not been for little Demelza's worried cry in the night ... who knows?

As a place to work in, Jess and I had managed to rent a condemned cottage in Back Road West. It consisted simply of one room down and one room up. We converted the bottom room into a pottery workshop and showroom, and the top into an office for myself. It was a quaint corner cottage, approached by a flight of stone steps, and when we hung a wrought iron sign outside, made by our friend Jack Richards, the whole effect was rather striking – at least I suppose so, for during that summer we had hundreds of holiday-makers coming up to take a look round.

This was our first experience of direct contact with customers and we viewed it with mixed feelings. On the one hand, especially early in the summer, there were many most interesting callers, intelligent and cultured people, who appreciated the art and craft of pottery, many of them from abroad. On the other hand, especially in August, there were floods of people who not only had no feeling for pottery but seemed incapable of knowing the difference between a hand-made article and a manufactured one (and in pottery there *is* quite a difference). The only time when the two kinds of visitors might be said to have a common meeting point was when Jess sat throwing at her electric wheel. Then everyone just stood and watched, with open-mouthed astonishment, this living revelation of a craft that is nearly as old as mankind itself.

It is at moments like this that I become more and more convinced that it is the artist and craftsman, rather than the politician, who may lead the world to its salvation. Art knows no barriers, whether national or racial – artists are unified by their common simple purpose.

After a tedious winter spent in Virgin Street we moved to a small cottage near the Wharf, and still we had not been able to find a permanent home. It was not for want of trying. By now I was haunting the estate agents, and we were continually inspecting potential houses. In such a mood we were nibbling at every conceivable bait. Converted landing craft at Lelant, old cottages out in the wilds of Trencrom, ex-Army huts on the Lizard – anything, anything in the world other than small rented cottages. Fortunately none of these scatter-brained ideas came to anything.

And then we took our walk along Porthmeor Beach. St Ives has several beaches, but of them all Porthmeor is the wildest and most beautiful, the least spoiled – oh, without doubt the most romantic. It is also one of the few beaches (I imagine anywhere) where the houses are literally on the beach, so that the sea comes surging right up to their back walls. It was along the soft sands of this beach, one spring afternoon, that Jess and I took a walk – if not weighed down with cares, at least feeling pretty worried. Should we buy somewhere out in the wilds? Should we commit ourselves to the adequate but somehow unattractive house in the back roads? We must do something, we couldn't go on living in other people's dolls' houses at huge holiday rents. Our capital was draining, we would have to borrow heavily anyway to buy anywhere.

'Ah,' said Jess dreamily. 'I know where I'd *like* to live ... where I've always wanted to live. There!'

We were at that moment just passing the glass doorway of the only house with a door which actually opened directly on to Porthmeor Beach. In days gone by, the sands had risen up and completely covered that door, but at last the council had put bulldozers at work and cleared away some of the mounds. Now you could walk off the sands straight through those glass doorways. At least you could have done if the doors had not been firmly bolted and shuttered.

We climbed on the single step which separated sand from door and peered in between the rows of shutters. Everything inside looked long and empty and unused; here and there a chair or table standing with a strangely unwanted, forlorn look. But it had not always been so.

'Do you remember,' said Jess, 'how it was ten years ago?'

Then these glass doors had stood wide open. Inside the impression was of an endless shadowy cavern, for the room extended indefinitely on and on (its actual measurement was, and is, some 65 feet). About half way down the room was the enormous oak side table that literally groaned under the weight of good things – plates of home-made scones, fruit cakes, shortcake biscuits, bowls of fresh fruit, jars of blackberry jam, slabs of cheese, pickles, onions, a hunk of ham, and a large shallow bowl of Cornish cream. All this, and heaven too, was offered ad lib – you were invited to help yourself to a second helping – for that mere 2s 6d a head. Little wonder that the restaurant was usually crowded: but there was more to it than that.

Mr and Mrs Keely with their kind hearts, and much too easy-going a disposition, were intuitively sympathetic to the artists of St Ives. One of their failings – or triumphs depending how you look upon things – was a tendency to give some of the poorer artists regular free meals. In theory this should have been covered by the revenue from normal holiday-makers, but somehow, this revenue was never as expected. Life there was always gay and amusing, with arguments in the kitchen until three in the morning, and people went off to the four corners of the earth vowing they would recommend all their friends to come and stay – yet somehow, things never went right financially. In the end, long after we had returned to London, we heard that the business had packed up, and the house was for sale. At the time we had exchanged knowing glances, but there was then nothing we could have done and eventually, we heard, the house was auctioned off. But often when we thought about St Ives we really thought of the St Ives which that house represented. Atlantic waves on your doorstep, a world of sunshine and sand and waves, and of artists at work, of a curious escape perhaps from reality – perhaps to reality.

Now we stood peering in at a lot of ghostly memories.

'It doesn't seem occupied,' said Jess.

I stepped back and looked upwards, spying curtains.

'Oh, I think it is, you know.'

We stepped back and looked about us. We knew that the house extended back a long way, and that the front entrance was in a road leading round to the sea. Of course it must be occupied, and no doubt was busily functioning as a guest house or something.

I looked at Jess, and then shrugged.

'Come on, let's be on our way.'

We tramped along the sands, and then walked up the slope that turned into Porthmeor Road. It was not really on our route to go along Porthmeor Road, but suddenly Jess spoke.

'There's no harm in just knocking at the door. You could ask.'

'Ask what?'

'Ask if the house is for sale, of course.'

As in the best story books, miraculously, it was. It would be tedious, and perhaps unwise, to go into the full ramifications of how we raised the money to buy St Christopher's, a process involving mothers, banks, solicitors, building societies and, in the end, even friends and acquaintances. The general reaction was disbelief, suspicion, scepticism. Building societies all clung stubbornly to a conviction that anyone buying a house with eight bedrooms must be going into the guesthouse trade: in vain we pointed out that we had six children and would be glad of the rooms. Banks on the other hand were impressed by the house, but less by our income and earning possibilities.

Mothers and friends, bless them, shared a little more of our own woolly and unfounded-optimism. Solicitors threw a cold light of reality upon the whole confusion of proceedings – sometimes too much, so that the whole deal seemed off. But in the end, though we could never feel really quite sure who owned the house, indubitably we were in possession.

The first day, like Army commanders planning a campaign, we allocated the troops. Martin and Gill, as the two elder children, were given the two largest bedrooms; Stephen and Jane received the two medium-sized rooms, and Demelza and Genevieve were, rather forcibly, ushered into one medium room.

'But the others have got rooms of their own!'

'I want a room of my own … I'm not going to sleep with Melza!'

'I don't want to sleep with Genny!'

There is a simple answer to this sort of fruitless argument. A bunk bed. The bunk bed we obtained was ex-Army type, probably rather uncomfortable, but it completely took Demelza's and Genny's minds off their bone of contention. For the next hour or two they climbed and jumped happily about their bunk bed, while we continued our dispositions.

Here perhaps a word or two about the layout of St Christopher's. It was an unusual sort of house, not attractive so much in itself or its shape, but for its position. Its front stood innocuously enough on a corner of Porthmeor Road, an ordinary gable type of front such as many suburban houses have. From that end the onlooker might simply see a house with two front rooms, on either side of the glass front door, and three bedrooms above. But once entered, the house began its surprises. The entrance room had a door at the far end which, when opened, revealed a vista of unending corridor, flanked with doors of innumerable rooms and meeting at the end with a door which on opening filled the place with light – for here was our own sitting-room looking right out upon the beach. Then again, turning right on entering, there was a short flight of stairs leading downstairs – and once again the long endless stretch leading to the light and the sea. On this floor, too, turning away from the sea, was a very large kitchen, so large that it defeated all efforts to make shape and sense of its odd proportions. It was indeed a kitchen with something of a history.

*

We were asleep when Martin called. It was, after all, about six o'clock in the morning. What he was doing up at that time I can't imagine: in the ensuing circumstances of the time it didn't seem to matter very much. Martin had a straightforward approach to disaster. Whereas Stephen, with a macabre twist of mind, liked to dwell on all kinds of hypothetical and horrible happenings: 'Fancy, if Demelza was run over by a steam-roller, who would bring me my breakfast:' – Martin simply got his pleasure out of announcing hard, stark, fearful facts.

'Dad,' called out Martin's clear, crystal-clear voice, suitably inflected with foreboding. 'You'd better come. The sea's in the kitchen.'

'Mmmmmmmm?' I said.

Beside me, Jess stirred angrily.

'For goodness sake tell him to shut up.'

'Yes,' I said. 'Do be quiet, that's a good boy. I can't think – '

'*Dad!*' shouted Martin through the keyhole, like a foghorn. 'Come quickly – it's everywhere!'

It was, too. In the kitchen, in the sitting-room, in the cafe one long endless sea of it, about six inches deep and for all we knew gathering depth every moment. Carpets were covered, books were awash, furniture was tilting, debris was accumulating everywhere. I stood half way down the stairs, still half asleep, staring upon this sudden transformation of a scene which I had left the previous evening, all spick and span and tidy. I could hardly believe my eyes: when I saw Martin and Stephen in Wellington boots, carrying buckets and heading for the sea door, I had to.

'Jess!' I called, weakly, unable to shoulder the burden alone. 'You'll have to come – The sea is in the kitchen.'

It took us two or three hours to deal with the crisis. Fortunately the tide, in the meantime, took a turn, as one might say, for the better. With the receding of pressure we were able to begin sweeping unwanted water, in long organized waves across kitchen, sitting-room, and cafe floor and out of the door on to the wet sands outside. The children all enjoyed it, joining in with the sort of will one would have welcomed on other less exciting occasions, such as washing up after dinner for eight. Martin took charge, uttering the orders, 'One, two, three – push! One, two three – push!' – Upon which Stephen, Gill, Jane, Demelza, and little Genevieve, armed with a variety of instruments from brushes to dust-bin lids, bent down and literally pushed the water on its way. There were deviations, of course, Stephen persuaded Demelza that there were strange fishes to be seen swimming around the fire-place, and when she bent down to see for herself, gave her a gentle but decisive push in. When he tried to do the same to Genevieve, Gill leaned across and clouted him. Thus was the jungle law preserved.

But in general the children were far too interested in this unusual and rather bizarre situation. So were Jess and I, though in a less happy-go-lucky way. We were worried less about the sea, as what would be left when the sea had departed. We had reason to be: the carpets were heavy and sodden with sea water … we were to waste several days trying to dry them off before outside advice, and the evidence of our noses, told us that this was not the right way to go about things.

'What you want to do,' said old Mr Ward, the carpenter from up the road, 'is to wash them down in fresh water – takes away the salt, you see.'

So then we had to get bucket loads of fresh water and carry them from the kitchen to the yard where we had hung up the now dry carpets and make them wet all over again – but really, that is another story.

We weren't insured, of course: we'd only been in the house a few days and hadn't got around to it. Still, it was some comfort later to find out that no insurance company would cover us against sea damage.

'I mean to say, would you?' said the insurance agent, leaning out of the back door and watching the Atlantic waves pounding up the beach. 'Would you, now?'

'Hey, come in,' I said hastily. 'Let's bolt the doors quickly.

We don't want the sea in again. I've just washed those damn carpets.'

*

It was impossible not to know that St Christopher's had been a guest-house, even though our purposes were more private. Every room was painted in the standardized and horrible chocolate brown and cream so beloved of conservative boarding-house keepers. Every room had its standard little wash basin, its standard little built-in-cupboard, its standard little lamp sockets. No doubt before the furnishings had gone, each had its standard little bed and its standard neat carpet. There even lingered about the rooms a curious aroma of past lettings, a sense of anonymous humanity, so that it was easy to close one's eyes and visualize the scenes.

But we were lucky. This was our home at last. We could make of it what we wished. And one of the first things we could do was to wash away the sad taint of these past days, to strip down the walls, to give a new coat of paint – to bring colour and life to a somewhat dowdy interior. We began work on the day we first moved in and with the aid of several good friends, achieved something of a transformation within a week. We stripped off wallpapers, painted walls white to give more light, did the woodwork in blackboard paint, hung up a few paintings we possessed – in the children's rooms some of their own efforts – and generally gave the place a new brightness.

Next we tried to sort out the living arrangements. Sharing small cottages with six children had merely enhanced our conviction that they needed a sitting-room – and so did we – and never the twain shall meet, or so we hoped. We had our room, a small but lovely sitting-room looking over the sea – but what about the children? For how long could they be left below, running up and down the 65-foot-long rooms, or worse, riding bicycles over the lovely wood floors? At one time indeed there seemed a danger of their taking over the whole of the lower floor. But we had to think of our own plans. Yet the children must have a general playroom. In the end we compromised, calling upon old Mr Ward, who with mystifying skill took a few sheets of hardboard and built a folding partition across the middle of the long room – one half making a room for the children – the other, seaward half, remaining intriguingly empty, to await our further plans.

In their room the children had an old-fashioned suite which we picked up in a sale for £2, a green cord carpet which would have seemed enormous anywhere else, but was rather lost in a room which still measured over thirty feet long, and a very long kitchen table with a renovated plywood top. Not a lot to go on, perhaps … but … enough. On the second day we found the covers off the couch and pinned on by tin tacks around the edges of the table.

'Big Chief Running Water's Tent,' said Demelza. Demelza was the Wild Western of our family. Where other children caught fish or went swimming or rode bikes, she became a Red Indian chasing or chased by cowboys. Sometimes she was also a cowboy, or maybe a Red Indian cowboy; but at all events she wore a holster, sometimes a feathered cap, and twiddled toy guns around her hands. As a pacifist and a supporter of nuclear disarmament I disapproved of all this, but was unable to explain things satisfactorily to Demelza. There appeared many good reasons why a girl of nine should not rush around brandishing a tomahawk and yelling out bloodcurdling threats – more reasons, for instance, than even against a boy doing such things. But Demelza remained unaffected by all arguments. Temporarily bereft of her hatchet or Colt, she would adopt another favourite role, old time boxer, rasing her bony little hands and banding them furiously. 'Come on now, do you want to box? Shall I box you?' Since the inevitable follow on to this was a flurry of windmill-like blows, all delivered with ferocity and force, I invariably used to take the coward's way of retreat: comforting myself with memories of Demelza crying out harrowingly at night because of some suspected shadowy movement, and clinging to me with her tiny trembling body.

Then there was the saga of the piano. I was at a furniture sale in Penzance and could not help noticing the pianos – there were in all six of them. Five did not even fetch a bid. The sixth and last one I could not resist, and it became mine for 5s; it was of course one of the old upright ones, but in quite reasonable condition. I went round to the nearest furniture remover and inquired the cost of transporting it nearly ten miles to St Ives. 'Three pounds,' he said. As there was no alternative, we arranged the deal. A day or two later we had to remove a large window pane and do some work with a hacksaw in order to get the piano into the children's room. Naturally, as is the way with these things, it was many months before we put back the window pane, and for some time the room was icy cold, until Martin thought of filling the space with an old suitcase. In the meantime the piano was installed, and a succession of small children, including most of our neighbours', took turns at trailing up and down with one, or maybe two fingers. We thought this was the most horrible sound we had heard, until later on Gill, who has a faintly musical ear, picked out a complete tune, 'Who's Sorry Now,' and played it over and over *and* over again. Fortunately after a period as part of a Red Indian ambush place, the piano suddenly went out of favour – only recovering its interest when Jane and some friends turned it into a shop counter, collecting all manner of objects which were stored inside the piano's innards.

A television set and an old gramophone completed the furnishing of the children's room, and no doubt provided them with much amusement. But nothing could compare with their favourite game – which was to slip into the farther end of what had once been the long room, open two glass doorways on to the beach, and then take high speed running long jumps out on to the sand. This was a game which attracted quite an enormous amount of both enthusiasm and followers. The latter, children of neighbours from all directions, accumulated into such numbers that often teams would be formed, and whole afternoons devoted to the famous St Christopher Long Jump. One of the great attractions, of course, was the element of the unknown: you could never be sure what unexpected hazard lay waiting outside. It might be a large Alsatian dog, a deckchair, an old lady with a parasol, several small children – or even, via Martin's sense of humour, a large hole dug in the sand and covered lightly with cardboard and sand. I was too old a hand to get caught by this one, but Jess one day practically disappeared down such a hole, and for some time afterwards could be seen grimly chasing Martin up and down the beach.

This particular beach game became much more popular, and twice as dangerous and exciting, later in the year when, following complaints by residents of the rising sand, the local council employed a bulldozer to clear away huge mounds. As a result our door was no longer level with the sand but some five or six feet *above* sand level. This would have necessitated urgent structural work had it not been that, much to our surprise, we discovered that there already existed a set of wooden steps. Evidently at some previous time the sands had been low, and these wooden steps which had been put in place had stayed there ever since. Now, having been buried in damp sand for some years, they were in a state of general rottenness, but they served for the moment, and we were able to concentrate on the new version of our game – jumping and clearing the steps.

This was really quite simple: the new excitement was that now, in addition to its being a long jump, it was also like the coming-down part of a high jump. You took off and soared through the air, and then down and down *and* down. I don't know how long the game might have gone on had it not been for the unfortunate day when three of the children chose to jump at the same time and landed in the middle of a serene picnic party of old ladies in wide-brimmed straw hats. None of them was seriously injured, but their subsequent legal claims convinced me that it was time to put an end to this particular fun and games, and I began applying restrictive practices, like fines.

What really finished things, however, was the disappearance of our steps. I have already indicated that our house stood on the very edge of the sea, and sometimes even succumbed to its entry. Many other times, however, the sea was frustrated, and its huge waves pounded in angry impotence against the stony foundations, splashing spray all over the glass doors, and even the windows above. It was on occasions like that that the sea, like any other bully who is thwarted, attempted to take it out of something else – in this instance, the weak link, our old wooden steps.

First the sea cunningly washed away huge mounds of sand, so that suddenly one day descending the steps, I was aghast to find them ending with space between the bottom spar and the sand. This meant that they were simply hanging on by their top attachment to the floor of the house. The next tide soon put an end to that. We watched out of the top window, unable to do anything, as one huge wave after another crashed against the steps, tugging them this way and that. Even so we did not really believe nature would win the battle. Later, we went to bed, though perhaps we slept uneasily.

In the morning, a local fisherman called round. 'Them your steps on the rocks?' Them were, alas, smashed to smithereens.

The effect of this, as I was saying, was to put a stop to the jumping game – not because any of the intrepid children were afraid to jump into space, but because they were all too lazy to make the long walk back to the front door, since with no steps it was impossible to come in the back way. In due course our old friend Arthur Slater, one of the Lamorna woodchoppers, made us another pair of steps – but by then, fortunately, the children had other interests.

Beside, we too had our plans. Already we were like some double-edged industrial automaton, myself tapping away daily at the typewriter, Jess in the next room grimly throwing pots – slaves to the eternal quest for money and more money with which to feed and clothe and keep our growing children. Sometimes it was quite frightening to pause, and then to realise that we dare not pause, that everything about our large family-life was geared up to a level where there was no prospect but work, work, and more work. It was bad enough for me at the typewriter, continually having to concoct new ideas for articles and books over and above those that I genuinely wanted to write (I don't want to imply that writers do not sometimes benefit from the crack-of-the-whip of a commission – but sometimes they like to pause a while). But it was worse for Jess, whose work was so essentially physical.

However, now we had plans for adding a third string to our output – we would continue the beach cafe at St Christopher's, serving ice creams and tea trays, and soft drinks, that sort of thing.

During the winter we cleared out the long room, and with the help of Mr Ward, our old carpenter friend, installed a smart modern snack bar, with urns and cookers and ice cream machines neatly laid out behind. We draped lengths of old fishing nets up and down the walls and over the ceiling and installed subdued lighting. A few visits to sales soon procured dozens of tables and chairs, and we spent long hours painting these all a simple bright red. Next came the ordering of cutlery and china plates, though Jess herself would be able to provide her own pottery coffee mugs and jugs.

We had no experience of running even a beach café, but it seemed simple enough, and in the long run so it was. As I was tied up with my own work and keeping an eye on the pottery showroom in the summer, and Jess herself would be fairly busy with pottery, she decided to take in a partner on the working side of the cafe. I am all against partnerships myself, from bitter experience, but at least Julian brought a lot of gaiety and amusement into our lives, along with a certain chaos. He was a flamboyant good-looking young man who would walk around St Ives in the evenings wearing a bright red cloak and a carnation in his lapel, usually with his curly fair hair tinted a light blue or green. This is such a dull and dreary world of ours that we should welcome and applaud those who have courage enough to stand out and carve a niche of their own, however bizarre.

Julian was staying at Trewyn, a large and gracious old manor house in the centre of St Ives, belonging to another friend of ours, John Milne, a sculptor. Most of our friends in St Ives tended to be artists of one kind and another. This might seem natural enough, since I am a writer and Jess a potter. But in St Ives the situation was somewhat complicated. Every summer art students from London flocked down, taking part-time jobs as waiters in cafes and thronging into the 'Sloop' and the 'Castle' at every opportunity. The result, at least in the summer, was a surfeit of painters so that the general public, not surprisingly, developed a certain antagonism to the rows of beatniks lining the harbour walls in the afternoon sunshine.

It was perhaps indeed a pity that so many beatniks and art students and would-be artists crowded into one small town, but

I do not think we should be too hasty in dismissing them. In this day and age of mass production and conveyor belts, atomic arms race and metropolitan rat races, what is unworthy about a desire to flee from it all to a place like St Ives, where there is not only the beautiful scenery and brilliant lights, but also the atmosphere well known to be sympathetic to the artist?

Which person is going to contribute most to the human good – the non-thinking semi-automaton of a man or woman who daily knocks rivets into a warship or equips a bomber aircraft or, dutifully wearing his radiation-proof mask, works on some terrible nuclear weapon – or a young, still idealistic (unwashed if you like) beatnik who merely wants to sing a song or write a poem or paint a picture?

I know whose side I am on, and the more I learn of the criminal actions and values of our so-called statesmen the less surprised am I to meet yet another pathetic escaper to the comparative peace of Cornwall. Of course it is no escape really: the bell tolls for us all and we cannot help hearing its mournful, warning peals. But at least if we attempt in our lives to be creative rather than negative, we are surely one step nearer salvation.

Living now in close contact with the artists of St Ives I returned to a task which I had begun during my *Cornish Review* days, namely the writing of a short history of the art movements in Cornwall. I do not mean an art criticism, for I am not a painter and had no wish to enter the already over-crowded field of art reviewing, with all its petty feuds. What had always fascinated me had been the physical effect of Cornwall upon artists, and this seemed to manifest itself most clearly in the case of painters and sculptors. There was also the subsidiary interest of the development of such a continental thing as an art colony, here in Britain. Accordingly I now began collecting material for a book which was eventually published, lavishly illustrated with photographs and reproductions, under the title of *Britain's Art Colony by the Sea*. In the book I tried to portray the gradual growth of the art colonies of West Cornwall over about seventy or eighty years, and at the same time to describe the different schools of painting culminating in the one now on the ascendant, the modernist abstract movement as represented by Barbara Hepworth, Ben Nicholson, Peter Lanyon, Bryan Wynter, Johnny Wells and others. No such record existed previously and I hoped that the book provided a useful introduction to any newcomer to the area. Some day, though, I should like to forget about art colonies and simply analyse the mysterious relationship between the artist at work in Cornwall, and the land and sea around him, covering not only painters, but poets and novelists, musicians and craftsmen, and so on.

Writing my book brought me closer into contact again with many old friends among the artists as well as new ones and imperceptibly we ourselves merged into the social life of the St Ives art colony. Although it can be beset by personal feuds and head-hunting ceremonies this life can have unity and familiarity which can be very sustaining and stimulating. There were many lively discussions in pubs, numerous parties in studios, or out at remote cottages, frequent amusing gatherings such as the annual fancy dress arts balls. Morally I do not think the life of St Ives was any better or worse than in other parts of the country: wives occasionally left husbands or vice versa, someone had an affair, someone ran off – but this happens all over the country. And in what I consider the important sense of the word 'moral,' St Ives was a more moral centre than many other places. Most members of what was called the art colony had thought enough about life to take a stand, to try to follow a conscious way of life, that of the artist. This meant, in most cases (not all, I agree) that there was a basic feeling for human values. It was, I think, no accident that artists were at the forefront of such movements as the Campaign for Nuclear Disarmament, the Abolition of Hanging, and various international friendship schemes. In many ways the artist is often the world's conscience, if only because he cannot help himself, and this must have its effect in personal relationships, which, though they may seem to outside eyes eccentric, are usually guided by honesty and integrity.

*

As that year drew near its close Jess and Julian fell out over a variety of cafe organizational problems, and we found it simpler to run the café on our own. But before the inevitable crisis there was a summer – indeed *that* summer, 1959 – that was almost idyllic. With the café steps leading right on to Porthmeor Beach, which is easily the nicest and least spoiled of St Ives beaches, the café soon became a centre for all our friends, apart from the hundreds of holiday-makers. As one sunny afternoon followed another, so the queues formed for ice creams and beach trays, and often we were forced to call extra help. Sometimes Gill and Jane performed very efficiently behind the ice cream counter, but the trouble with children and a café was that supplies mysteriously diminished. We soon came to the conclusion that with six children in the same house as unlocked supplies of sweets and ice creams and other delectables, a certain percentage must be allocated for 'Losses.'

What was pleasant about the café was that, owing to its unusual situation, it was impossible to pretend all was work and no play. There were always slack periods, or times when a friend would take over, and then Julian and Jess and the children and I would slip on our bathing costumes and run down to the waiting waves. 'Waiting' was hardly the adjective to describe the average Porthmeor sea. Our beach faced north, and consequently took the full force of various north or north-east winds, while there were several fast and powerful currents. As a result at almost any time of the day or night there were long powerful waves surging over the vast flat sands.

And this brings me, quite naturally, to surfing. In our household surfing became what perhaps watching football matches or following the dogs or collecting stamps was to another. That wonderful golden summer, we all became surf-happy. As it happened part of the café trade was hiring out surf-boards, so we could usually find a board (for Stephen we even had a smaller board made). Thus armed we would stride out into the frothing seas – to embark on one of the world's most delightful and exhilarating pastimes.

I find it difficult to describe the art of surfing in words. It is, I sometimes think, almost a mystical experience – indeed more than once, on an early summer evening at Porthmeor with the tide coming in in vast long rollers, I found myself with several other surfers, strangers perhaps, and caught us glancing at each other with a kind of wonder in our eyes as we picked ourselves up after soaring in like birds in flight. Perhaps flight in the form of gliding, or maybe skiing – perhaps these are the nearest analogies.

It is impossible really to teach surfing, it is just a question of practice, practice, practice. At first you may flounder and splash and even temporarily be bowled over, but don't despair. Always try to catch a wave just before it breaks so that you are swept in triumphantly on the crest of its journey. To do this judge approximately at what point the wave is likely to break, position yourself there, holding the slim surf-board in front of you with the bottom and tucked into the pit of your stomach and your hands at full stretch, gripping the top ends of the curve. Wait until the wave is almost on you and about to break – then fling yourself forward.

It is, I suppose, a little like loving – or indeed living. And if I had to search for ten years I do not think I would find a more fitting image to describe our family existence at St Ives. Our life was rather like an eternal surfing – an endless launching ourselves into the unknown in the hope that we would be carried onwards towards the shore. Experience might teach us that perhaps that shore would never quite be reached, but it had at the same time made us more proficient in the craft itself. We learned the value of several sources of revenue, however fluctuating: when the writing failed, there was the pottery, when the pottery was out of demand, there was suddenly the summer beach café, and so on. It all made life a complicated and chaotic affair. If you can perhaps imagine the following things all happening at once under one (admittedly long) roof: a pottery furnace glowing, wheel spinning, tyepwriter tapping, café heater booming and clanking, four radios blaring, dogs barking, cats miaowing, old cars spluttering, hamsters gone broody, unexpected visitors, phone ringing, and children, children, everywhere (some not even our own) – then you have some idea of the daily situation as it used to be at St Christopher's.

It was a situation that must often have seemed to outsiders complete chaos and almost unbearable, and of course often it seemed an eternity since I sat in my little Trencrom cottage peacefully brooding ... But then there is, as always in life, the reverse side to the coin; when Jess and I used to look out of a window and see our sun-tanned children running happily into the sea, or watched their bright-eyed faces sitting around one of the eight birthday teas of the year, or perhaps turned and surveyed them, in bewildered amazement, all squashed into the back of a very old car ... That sort of thing, I suppose could almost compensate for such traumatic moments as: 'Dad, you'd better come! The sea's in the kitchen!'

II

The Trouble with Teenagers

Summers at St Christopher's meant a chance of some extra income from either pottery or the beach café ... in winter time the ship had to be kept afloat by the pen, or rather to be precise, the Olympia typewriter. The image is not a loose one. Ah well, people always say to us when we bemoan the difficulties of keeping going, at least you're lucky, you have the children. Jess and I stare at them in hollow-eyed incredulity or perhaps burst out into maniacal laughter, depending on the mood we are in at the end of a trying day.

After all, you don't have to be a brilliant mathematician to work out some of the permutations. A family of eight may well need three times eight meals a day, say two times eight sets of clothes, two times eight sets of sheets, blankets, at least eight chairs and a table big enough for eight, couches and armchairs for eight, and so on. That is only the beginning of the complications of large family life. Rooms are needed, beds are needed, living space is needed – and then there is the problem posed by the different requirements of different age groups. All our lives Jess and I have been like fugitives from the Martians, as represented by our children.

For some years we fondly deluded ourselves that there would be a golden era when the older children were, well, older. We even indulged in dreams of lying back with our feet up being waited upon by grateful, thoughtful teenagers. Life has not been like that, alas. The only cups of tea we have had made for us were usually by the two youngest, Demelza and Genevieve, than which hardly anything more horrible can be imagined, though the thought sweetens the taste.

By a strange quirk of fate I was an only child myself, then I became that stage-joke, father of six. I often used to try and remember what life was like in a family of three, but somehow I could not recapture the halcyon image. I was left with the grim reality of the jungle warfare of large family life. At St Christopher's we felt from the beginning we were there to stay, and consequently we devoted quite a lot of thought to the allocation of house space. Fortunately the children were all able to have a room each except the two youngest – of whom Demelza campaigned continually at the older children: 'Martin, when are you going away?' – 'Gill, will you be getting married soon?' – with one eye on their rooms. The two largest rooms downstairs, the kitchen and a large sitting-room, were declared a kind of no man's land where the whole family had equal rights, the sitting-room being a kind of common-room for all the family but, since it included the television, containing certain rights for parents who wanted to watch a few of the programmes.

Just one room in the house, the small lounge on the floor above, looking directly over the sea, was kept apart as Jess and Denys's room. It was the furthest point away from children and the kitchen and television and every other reminder of family life, and we guarded it jealously. Here we could have our own friends, usually other married couples with whom we commiserated about respective family problems. However, to get to this room our friends had to travel along a corridor some 50 feet long, with doors opening off to various children's rooms, and they were lucky if they reached us intact. More likely they would have had to admire one child's new dress and another's drawings, and probably read a fairy tale to a third.

Jess and I were both determined from the start that so far as possible our relationship with our children should be on a free and equal basis. That is, we abhorred the Victorian trend of harsh punishments and authoritarian, often false values. In our family everyone spoke his or her mind without fear or favour, and while there were the inevitable ups and downs of family life, and the usual quarrels and jealousies between sister and sister, brother and brother, older and younger, I don't think the result has been too bad so far as developing individual personalities is concerned. Each of our children seems to me a personality in his or her own right, and a pretty independent one at that.

The one advantage of this fairly free way of life, where we have always encouraged the children to fend for themselves – from an early age they could all, even the youngest, cook for themselves if need be – is that the children do seem better equipped for standing on their own feet and facing the world. For instance, the older children were quite capable of travelling from one end of the country to the other, usually by the favourite teenage method of hitch-hiking. They had all kinds of adventures and met all kinds of people, and I can't believe that this experience did them any harm. It is really quite interesting how our modern youngsters automatically adapt themselves to this more travel-conscious age. They think nothing, for instance, of hitching from St Ives to Taunton, or even to Richmond, London, for a one-day jazz festival. Their friends are often scattered all over the country and there are cryptic phone calls. 'Llewellyn's at Ringwood this week-end, but he'll be down at Mevagissey after that' – 'Pete's at Danny's in London, but he'll be back on Tuesday – then we're all going to Pete's at Exeter.'

At first Jess and I used to look forward to the time when our older children entered the semi-grown up era of the teenager. I don't quite know what we imagined, but possibly at the back of our minds was some vague idea of birds flying gaily from the nest, the brave little dears going out into the world, that sort of thing. It wasn't like that, somehow; and if it is going to be it seems to be taking an awful long time. Meantime, instead of the birds flying gaily from the nest we found quite the reverse – other birds came flying into our nest instead. Almost everything that happened to us through our unwilling involvement in the world of teenagers and beatniks – and it sometimes seemed like a nightmare – was summed up for me one day when I heard one teenage friend saying to another: 'Come on, let's go down to *Martin's* house.' (My italics.) I suppose one might say that the difference between a child and a teenager is that the latter *consciously* seeks to take possession of the home.

At first, as I say, Jess and I headed like innocents to the slaughter. 'Bring your friends home if you want to' – 'Wouldn't Charlie like to stay the week-end?' – 'Yes of course Belinda can come down for a few days.' It wasn't, to be honest, that we particularly wanted any of these situations. Both of us worked hard and we had no help and had to cook all meals and look after the children and the house, and we usually dreaded the arrival of another person, especially if not one of our own friends. But we felt we owed it to our children: they should be able to bring their friends home if they wished.

At first things didn't seem too bad. At the age of fifteen Gill had local girl friends from her school, they would all sit up in her room giggling and making up and swapping stories about boy friends. Martin had fellow football players in his room browsing through *Charles Buchan's Football Annual* or playing Monopoly. Jane was as yet too young really to be interested, or to introduce yet more problems by seeking to do everything her older brother and sister did, though three years younger. No, things weren't too bad.

Then – abruptly it seemed, but in fact it must have been over a few months – the teenagers-cum-beatnik period was upon us. Martin's hair, never very short, grew down to his shoulders: his trousers disappeared to be replaced by strange drainpipe jeans and in place of his normal shoes, high leather bootees. Gill, for her part, while still applying five coats too many of mascara to her eyes, now dressed in winkle-pickers, jeans which had been soaked to shrink so that they appeared welded on to her not unshapely frame, and either one of Martin's jerseys or mine, whichever she could pinch on the quiet. Not long afterwards an even stranger apparition appeared, Jane with her hair grown three feet long so that it could be tucked into a leather belt round her waist, and clad in jeans like Gill's, shoes like Gill's and shirts like Gill's.

Jess and I viewed these goings on at first with an inane kind of indulgence. Well, we had all been rebels ourselves, we could understand all this, quite natural. Mmmm yes, it was rather difficult explaining to the headmaster of Martin's grammar School and as for the headmistress of Gill's grammar school – well, I had better draw a veil over their relationship. At least somehow the two girls were persuaded not to attend school in their new get-up, but at the boys' school the sixth-formers were to some extent allowed to dress as they wished, and

Martin was merely one of a group who extorted this liberty so casually offered.

Gradually, I won't say subtly, but rather with a kind of furtive discretion, our house began to take on strange new dimensions. I should like to choose exactly the right simile to describe what happened: I would say that the development was a *spiral* one. It began with the few, it ended with the many. In the beginning were the few. By a strange coincidence Martin's form-mates and friends were two more Bakers, Jonathan and Llewellyn Baker, sons of Frank Baker, by another coincidence also an author (probably best known for his classic comedy, *Miss Hargreaves*).

If I say that Llewellyn went about in sheepskin waistcoat turned inside out and an Ascot top hat with a small white mouse on the inside of the brim, and that Jonathan favoured an even larger and woollier coat and grew his hair possibly half an inch longer than Martin's, I am casting no aspersions on their potentialities to rise to the top of some future Establishment – but I am, perhaps indicating the general flavour of what here I might call Martin's circle. What linked Martin and Llewellyn and Jonathan was that they were all ardent supporters of the Campaign for Nuclear Disarmament (about which I write more fully in a later chapter) and this did give them some kind of basic reality in our lives. After all more than once we marched alongside them in parades or sat side-by-side on sit-downs.

They also had a group of fellow young CND'ers over at Mevagissey, and soon visits and counter-visits – mostly, we couldn't help feeling, visits – were taking place. It went something like this. We would all be sitting down to a nice quiet peaceful meal of two grown-ups and six ravenously hungry children. Here I might interpolate a necessary explanation that the mere administration of such a meal proved most complex, as there were invariably five knives, four spoons, eight forks, and an odd teaspoon or so to fill up the gaps: no matter how many knives, forks or spoons we bought, these were immediately lost in the sand or down innumerable cracks in floorboards and other places one would have thought impervious to cutlery. It was just as well we had a pottery of our own so that in extremis we could provide our own crockery – on the other hand more than one visitor about to raise a cup of tea to her lips was astonished to have it whipped away to make up a set going for sale upstairs.

Suddenly as we came purposefully down the staircase outside our kitchen, our eagle ears would detect the ominous heavy thud of visitors. (Our kitchen was underneath the entrance room to St Christopher's, and we became expert at guessing people's identities by their respective footfalls – in general, the footsteps of unknown visitors somehow always sounded heavy and ominous). At the doorway there would now appear one shadowy enormous figure after another – boys in duffle coats, girls in regulation black jeans, boys with curly hair and rings in their ears, girls with showers of frothy hair sweeping down to their knees. Squeals of delight from the younger children at the prospect of fun baiting their immediate elders, looks of dismay on the lined faces of the two older Val Bakers, sheepish grins from Martin and Gill and Jane. 'Hullo, Vicky. Hullo, Zonga. Hullo, Maud. Hullo, Janet. Hullo, David.'

While these exchanges were going on the newcomers were depositing rolled-up sleeping bags, crumpled rucksacks – and, of course, themselves – around the kitchen, which began to resemble the inside of an air-raid shelter during a raid in the last war. Next we would become conscious of a sense of strange but uncomfortable pressure: it got stronger and stronger, more and more obvious – at last, uneasily, Jess and I gobbled up the remnants of our meal and abjectly fled. We knew when we weren't wanted.

For some reason this sort of visitation usually happened on a week-end, and it is not exaggerating a great deal to say that if at any time for the next twenty-four hours we should pop down for anything we would find the same dozen or so slouched figures humped around the table, wreathed in circles of tobacco smoke (it is one of our minor martyrdoms that we don't smoke). During the night, of course, the bodies would be spread around a little more – some in the television room, some on the floors of various bedrooms and so forth. We never quite knew who slept where, but when once timidly we

ventured to suggest that perhaps it was a question of who slept
with whom we were rounded on fiercely -- 'We're not like *that,*
how old-fashioned you are. We're just good friends.' Which of
course was patently true; apart from the inevitable skittishness
and mild flirtations the main relationship between the
teenagers was obviously a kind of camaraderie of youth. We
knew – we could hear the cameraderie going on into all hours
of the night, interspaced with sudden blares of jazz from
Luxembourg or any other station which could be coaxed into
action in the middle of the night. Not that the teenagers
particularly needed radios, it seemed that every other one of
them carried a record player in his or her voluminous
rucksack. Martin, of course, had one, and at the peak of his
'pop' craze, I think 150 pop records – fortunately later his taste
changed to traditional jazz. Night after night we would hear
Martin's record player plodding through the repertoire in his
bedroom, which fortunately we had put as far away from us as
possible. In those days we used to feel sorry for our next door
neighbour who would appear periodically with a pathetic
request for Martin to turn down the volume. Later – when
Martin, who fancied himself as an amateur electrician, found
an old loudspeaker and connected up his player with a tiny
radio set in Gill's room across the corridor so that the volume
seemed to be doubled – we began to feel sorry for ourselves.

After a while our hearts would sink when word came of the
impending arrival of 'the Mevagissey lot,' as one group of
Martin and Gill's friends were known. They usually arrived in a
flotilla of motor scooters and cars borrowed from parents, and
since the journey was a fairly long one of fifty miles or so, it was
a reasonable supposition that they had come for at least a
night. Mind you, they had their saving graces. Many of the girls
were fresh-faced and pretty and bubbling over with life, and
even a tired old father could feel pleasantly revived and much
younger, just talking with them. But the overall effect was one
of exhaustion, mental and physical exhaustion – for us, I
mean, not the teenagers. For them exhaustion was an unknown
term. The talk was the thing, allied with the twist or some other
equally active expression.

At Christmas-time we hit on what we thought would be a

brilliant idea to work off the teenagers' steam. We let it be known that they could have a Christmas party at St Christopher's. In the past every Christmas we always had one large children's party for our six children, but by now it had become sadly obvious that the three older children had slightly different interests to the younger ones, so we decided we would have a small party for the 7-11 group, and a teenage party for the older ones. We said we would leave the party entirely in the hands of Martin, Jane and Gill – they could ask approximately six friends each, get in a barrel of cider, and organize things as they liked. We acknowledged that such a party could reasonably expect to go on until quite late and we went one better still – we announced that we ourselves would actually spend the night elsewhere. This was really a precautionary move for our own health's sake, as we could just imagine a night in St Christopher's with a teenage party in full swing (alas, as we were to discover a year or so later, our imagination was limited in scope). So off we went to spend a pleasant evening with our friends Anthony and Christianne. Earlier in the evening we did indulge in a little celebration drink in the Sloop with one or two friends, and coming out we decided to take a peep in at St Christopher's. Everywhere upstairs was quiet, but from downstairs came a vast hum of noise, voices and music hopelessly intermingled, one or two high spirited shrieks. We looked nervously down the stairs, but all was in darkness – we decided to leave well alone and tip-toed away to have a quiet elderly cup of coffee, and an uninterrupted sleep in Anthony and Christianne's spare room.

In the morning, feeling very refreshed, we had a pleasant stroll around the harbour before collecting the Sunday papers and heading homewards. We felt pretty sure everyone would still be asleep after the party, and wondered quite what amount of damage might have been done. We found the front door open and went in quite gaily; after all it was a bright Sunday morning, the party was over so the teenagers would depart, all was well with the world ...

'Listen,' said Jess, tugging at my arm. We both came to a tense stop. 'Do you hear?'

'Music,' I said grimly.

'And dancing,' said Jess in a hollow voice.

'And music,' I said more grimly.

'And shouting and laughing and – and – '

We looked at one another horrorstruck. No, it couldn't – it couldn't still be going on?

'I can't face it,' said Jess. 'I'm going to sit down here. *You* must go and find out.'

I started towards the top of the stairs and then stopped. I felt myself unable to face the sudden vision of that long room and all the ghastly sights it might contain. No, I decided, I would be discreet, I would go round the side entrance, into the kitchen.

When finally I let myself into the kitchen I found it comparatively quiet, there were only eight or nine teenagers there. One of them, Paul, a bespectacled boy in a red corduroy coat whom I knew, and who seemed to me more mature than most of them, looked at me with smiling pity.

'It's still going on,' he said. 'Look, I'm just making some coffee. Would you like some?'

I decided I had better have some – black. While I sipped it I culled a brief report from Paul which re-assured me that nothing drastic had happened.

'But – ' He shrugged and nodded in the direction of the long room, from which blared the familiar old pop tunes. 'Well, it's still going on.'

And so it went on, on and on, all through Sunday morning and Sunday lunch and Sunday afternoon and Sunday too and even into the beginning of Sunday evening …

'Don't you think … ?' began Jess.

'It's really time … ' I added.

'You all went home?' we said in unison, summoning up ancient echoes of parental authority.

Gradually, and no doubt sadly, the tireless teenagers came to the end of their week-end session. Just to speed the parting guests a little we gave two of them a lift out on to the A.30 at Hayle. It was getting a little dusky and I had some misgivings about how they would get on with hitching a lift at this time.

'Don't you worry,' said Belinda, cheerfully, lifting one black-jeaned leg out of the car. 'We'll be there in no time.'

And they no doubt were, for we had hardly stopped our car when a large saloon caught sight of Belinda's languid wave and pulled up with a jerk. As we turned round to head home we saw them zooming away at 60 miles an hour towards Mevagissey.

After this the pace of our visitations seemed to increase – so much so indeed that, perhaps moved by a sense of life-preservation, we began to protest.

'Don't your friends have homes of their own?'

'I don't suppose *their* mothers and fathers get swamped like this.'

'Couldn't *you* possibly go away this time?'

Briefly at one period came a blessed relief. The parents of one group of children, the Kittos, moved into a large country house at St Ewe near Mevagissey. We began hearing stories about the marvellous situation. Why, there was even a lodge-cottage that was empty. Our ears pricked up, but we were no quicker than our teenagers. The next weekend our house was miraculously empty: they had all gone to St Ewe where they spent a wonderful week-end taking over the Lodge.

'It was smashing, fabulous, had the place all to ourselves. We had a real ball.'

'But how did you manage?'

'Oh, easily.'

'Who did the cooking?'

'Why, Gill mostly.'

Jess and I looked, feeling faint, at Gill, aged seventeen, who in holiday times arose at mid-day each day and possibly contributed to the household domestic chores twice a year. Gill did the cooking? What were things coming to?

Still it wasn't for us to argue. We felt almost deliriously happy. They had found a new 'pad' (we were getting up in our terminology). Hooray!

'You'll be off to Mevagissey again this week-end, I expect?'

'Yes. It's absolutely fabulous.'

This honeymoon period lasted a month or so during which time I'm afraid we spared little thought to the tribulations of the Kittos who, we gathered gradually, seemed to be getting overrun with teenagers and were now even taking to cooking them meals. Perhaps we should have been kinder in our thoughts, for suddenly almost as abruptly as it started the Mevagissey phase seemed to come to a stop. Soon Martin and Gill were back in their rooms playing pop records and entertaining friends ...

III

Ice-Creams and Attics

Life with the children during our ten years at St Christopher's, as I have already indicated, was invariably chaotic, often exasperating, usually exhausting, but at least never dull. For a large part of the time, of course, there was the blessed weekday routine. Every morning the six would arise, one by one, eat hurried breakfasts and depart – though even in the manner of their departure they were hardly discreet. One by one they would storm into our bedroom and demand various intricate sums of money for bus fares, school lunches, etc., always culminating with a mysterious 3d piece which each had every day, presumably as some kind of symbolic protection.

However, at last the moment would come when the final boot had thundered over the showroom floor, the glass door had banged with reverberating echo for the sixth and last time – and a marvellous peace would descend over our battered old house. This was our halcyon period when Jess and I would creep down to the peace of the deserted kitchen and have a quiet cup of coffee and a perusal of the day's usual post; a golden hour before rumblings above indicated the arrival of someone to work in the pottery (or maybe even an early customer in the shop), or else some minion for the café.

Our beach café had staggered from one uneasy season to the next, and then a third, and after that Jess had washed her hands of it. Probably unwisely, I had decided to have one more go at the thing, and this time to utilise the raw material of our own personal employment pool: in other words, Martin, free for the long summer vacation.

Jess gave an expressive, indeed an eloquent shrug which somehow summed up her general feeling about both Martin

102

and myself as potential café proprietors.

'Go ahead if you want to – but don't say I didn't warn you.'

Ironically, our positions were reversed. Jess who had once been so enthusiastic about the café now saw all the snags and was forever reminding me of them. Perversely, the more she went on the more falsely optimistic, and tortuously experimental I became.

'I've been thinking – what's wrong is that everything's top heavy. Fancy having to do such a huge turnover and employ four people all for the sake, in the end of perhaps a couple of hundred pounds. Why in the time you've wasted on worrying about the café you could probably have made that much more making pottery. It's just all top-sided. No, I've got a better idea. We'll reverse the procedure. Cut down the café to the minimum, make it like a little kiosk, just serving ice creams and soft drinks and sandwiches – something that one person can manage on his own.'

'What about teas? Surely you'll do teas?'

I made an irritable gesture, wiping teas off the map for one half of the people on Porthmeor beach.

'No, it's just not possible. They'll have to drink lemonade and pop.'

'You're mad. Nobody will come.'

Well, of course, we did lose a bit of business over the teas, no doubt, but then once you have got settled on a nice spot on a beach it needs an awful lot of will power to get up and walk a quarter of a mile or so to the other end just for a cup of tea. Most of our customers did as I expected, and settled for a cold drink. Then there were always the ice cream and sandwiches and sweets … oh, yes, things would be all right.

For a couple of weeks before opening time Martin and I experimented with formations of what was left of the old counter and the three fridges and a cooler, arranging them in various permutations. Each time we got them set up in some semblance of order Jess would come down the stairs and complain that we were ruining the rest of the room or blocking the way to the sea, and we had to start all over again. Finally we hit on an agreed L-shape in one corner, which provided easy access for the customer bounding up the steps yet barred his progress further into the room. Against the wall opposite the counter we lined up our surf boards and wind-breaks, which we hired out day by day.

It was my eldest son's first paid job, and for that matter my first employment of anyone, and we viewed our new relationship with mutual suspicion.

'Martin, you will remember you're working now. Have to get up in the mornings, you know.'

'Yes, yes. Look, how can we make a profit if you keep taking a tin of bitter lemon? Can I have one?'

'Yes, well, within moderation, Martin. Now you won't forget, will you, to get in cut bread, ham, butter, that sort of thing. And what about some signs? You're good at lettering, I shall expect something striking. And then the surf boards need painting and then numbering. And the windbreaks.'

Martin's answer, as to everything that involved anything really strenuous apart from playing football or marching to Aldermaston, was a kind of strangled groan. I would tell myself that I mustn't stand over him and bother him, and I would go away and try not to come back for a couple of hours – when I did so there would be a faint suggestion of the café having been tidied up, and Martin would laboriously be scripting out, in rather unsuitable gothic lettering, a menu for the café.

'That's all very well, Martin, but what about the surf boards? And the windbreaks?'

Somehow, in a vague sort of way, we opened up. To my relief it seemed that Martin was able to operate the ice cream scoop, and indeed took a certain sporting pride in the number of ice creams he could serve in a day. Unfortunately it never seemed to penetrate that unless he modified the generosity of his helpings we would actually be selling ice cream at a loss. Opening bottles of pop also came easily into his province, and he let the customers reach for their sweets themselves, so that was no problem. Sandwiches, on the other hand were. After a couple of days when he made quite a few and hardly any were sold Martin dug his heels in and refused to waste money on buying materials for sandwiches that no one ate.

'Well, look, just make a couple, just for the look of the thing,' I said anxiously. 'After all those huge plastic containers look rather silly standing there empty.'

Martin condescended to do this, but whether he cast a malevolent spell on them or not, I never knew, but from that day on – sandwiches which in previous years so far as I knew had always gone quite well – practically stopped selling.

'Cigarettes would,' he said morosely. 'I get asked for cigarettes a lot.'

'Yes, and what's the profit on cigarettes? A halfpenny! it's just not worth it.'

Still we consoled ourselves, there were always the sweets. We eyed the imposing stacks of Crunchies and Picnics and Nutty Bars and Fruit Bars and Whirls and goodness know what else. Every morning in fact, when we came down into the cafe we eyed those piles – with increasing suspicion.

'Martin, do you get the impression there are fewer Crunchies than there were last night?'

'Yes, I blooming well do. And some of the Fruit and Nuts have gone, too.'

Sadly I was forced to the conclusion that the profits of my café were being endangered from within. Grubby little hands found it impossible to keep away from tempting bars of chocolate. In vain did I appeal to noble instincts, moral values and so forth: the answer always was a hurt look, a bland smile, a vehement promise. But the piles, subtly, kept receding.

After several weeks, in desperation – since the profit margin was fairly small, and non-existent with the present rate of absconding, I whittled down my café's scope still further. Indeed, by the time August came we were serving nothing, absolutely nothing, except ice cream and soft drinks, with hiring out boards and wind breaks as accessory means of raising that profit which somehow, even by my calculations, was not working out to plan.

There were other troubles too. While I could hardly expect Martin to look on the job with much excitement I was hardly prepared for the methods with which he chose to pass the long hours of waiting which often occurred on dull days. These were two-fold: one was to plug in his record player and play ceaselessly his collection of 100 pop records (superseded later in the season by New Orleans jazz, a slight improvement). The other was to accumulate in the café or I should say rather in the vast space beyond the café, occupied partly by tables and chairs left over from previous years – a growing, collection of beatnik friends. We were quite willing to believe that everything he said about them was true, they were nice and intelligent and interesting and so on. 'But why do they have to *sit* all day in the café? It's sunny outside, couldn't they sit on the beach? Besides, they – '

With some difficulty I stopped myself from suggesting that by their mere quantity the beatniks possibly put quite a lot of people off from coming in the café at all. At a time when they were very much being picked on in St Ives I didn't want to be party to any kind of discrimination! Yet the fact remained, I well knew, and they were one of innumerable reasons why, to my exasperation and Jess's grim knowingness, the café steadily went down and down. No tea, no cigarettes, no sweets, no cakes, no anything except ice cream and pop – and beatniks and endless dreary pop tunes ad infinitum – and then Martin, the most tired and weary café partner ever in creation – no, I suppose it is hardly surprising that business was no good. Even the windbreaks proved to be of very inferior make and kept sagging sadly, so that we spent much of the time buying tacks and furiously repairing them. Added to this was there worst of all the summers we had spent in Cornwall, raining day after day, windy afternoon after windy afternoon, even in sunny weather. Only the surfboards went gaily on their way, costing no money, bringing in the only sure profit of each day – but enough to pay Martin's dubiously earned wages.

Towards the end of August even Martin lost heart altogether and decided to go away to Mevagissey for the last couple of weeks and Jane, then fifteen, officiated at the last two weeks – on a dying fall as they say – of our doomed beach café. At last the ice cream man came for the last time, we ordered a last few hesitant gallons, same with the drinks; one Sunday in September Jane served out the last scoop, we sold off several surf boards, and we closed the cafe; leaving ourselves with a legacy of 24 tins of bitter lemons, a few raspberries and lemonades, and some empty fridges, and a forlorn fluttering flag: 'Try our Top Ten.' Watched carefully by a caustic Jess I did a final tot up of my books for the season.

'Well I must say in theory we have actually made a profit – a book profit, so to speak – about a hundred pounds, in fact. Not bad really if you remember that we didn't have to lay out lots of money or employ a staff of four. However … ' I frowned in puzzlement, 'I don't quite understand it, really, because I still have bills outstanding of nearly £80 and – well, there doesn't seem any money left to pay them.'

*

Soon after that episode Martin was accepted as a student at the Falmouth Art School and left for digs in Falmouth – the first of our six actually to leave home. I had a shrewd idea he was not altogether sorry to leave, because Martin has always been the lone bird of the family, preferring to pursue his own solitary course. As it was, he was able to come home every weekend, so that there was no final break.

Martin's departure meant among other things, what might be called a domestic promotion for the other young male member of the family. Stephen had for a long time coveted Martin's much larger bedroom, and naturally enough he quickly moved into the vacant room. Stephen was now fourteen and, we felt fondly, growing up: so we bought him some new curtains and a carpet and decorated the room, and encouraged him to have his friends up. Little did we know the fresh troubles we were nurturing! – for Stephen was a very different kettle of fish to Martin, a much more sociable sort, who not only took over that saying I have quoted, 'Come up to *my* house,' but did so, you might say, in a really big way.

The key to what might be called Stephen's Attic period of our later life at St Ives, was, precisely, the Attic. When we moved into St Christopher's, we had noted there were two attics, one a very long low one over the 65 foot restaurant (it was also 65 feet long, but only about 3 feet high, and so not much use except to dwarfs) – and another over the top three bedrooms. This second attic was quite a large lofty affair, and periodically Jess and I would put up a small ladder and climb up and move gingerly across the open beams, thinking thoughts about big studio rooms, dormer window and so forth. However, living in a house of such vast proportions as St Christopher's, where even with six children every one had their own bedroom, extension seemed rather pointless.

Until, that is, Stephen became interested in what almost immediately became 'his' attic.

'It only wants a floor laying – me and my friends Nicky and Oliver and Pete could do it ourselves quite easily.'

'But what about – well, planning permission, that sort of thing!'

'Nobody will ever know.'

'Well … '

In the end Stephen kept on so much that we agreed reluctantly to pay the cost of purchasing the necessary number of planks to lay a floor, and one day a big lorry from Harvey's drove up and deposited them outside the front door. Knowing that inquisitive eyes of not too friendly neighbours would be watching we hastily carried the load indoors out of sight and (Stephen and all those mythical friends needless to say, being away at school), got the planks up into the attic.

'Well, that's it – I wash my hands of things from here on,' I said grimly, not expecting much else to happen.

There I did the boys an injustice. Week-end after week-end they arrived, not only the ones Stephen had mentioned, but other strange tousled-haired boys, with names like Ian and Trevor and Harry and John, they would file sheepishly through the showroom and clatter up the stair and then acrobatically swarm up the one slender ladder and disappear into the Attic. Soon we would hear thumping and banging and we surmised that work must be in progress.

It was, too, to such good effect that after a couple of weeks, Jess and I were persuaded to venture up to see progress – which turned out to be quite considerable. There was now a gleaming, Bourn-sealed floor of deal planks, and the beginning of a large room measuring some 24 feet long by the same width, though the latter sloped down to a small headroom under the gables on each side.

'Just about enough room to sleep in down the sides,' we said jokingly, little realising the significance of our words.

Light was the next problem. There was none at all except a

single electric bulb on a long lead from the floor below.

'A couple of small dormer windows in the roof,' said Jess thoughtfully. 'That wouldn't be difficult.'

It wasn't, fortunately. Now Stephen's attic had a floor and daylight, and electric light if wanted – the next thing was furnishings.

'Well, we've one or two old mattresses,' we proffered hesitantly.

'Fine,' said Stephen, eyes gleaming. 'My friends will bring some too, and a couple of old couches.'

'By the way,' we asked curiously. 'Just exactly what – ?'

'Why, don't you know?' said our second son cheerfully. 'This is going to be my club. Don't you think it's a marvellous idea?'

Stephen's Club. The mere repetition of the words brings the memories flooding back. They are not altogether catastrophic memories by any means. At that time Stephen was working hard for O levels at the Humphry Davy Grammar School, Penzance, and had gathered around him a lively gang of boys like himself, all bright and intelligent. I suppose the number was about half a dozen, and they were banded together by many things, of which the Attic Club was obviously the most important.

There was also the famous car. This was a very ancient American Essex tourer, vintage, or positively veteran, which had belonged to Jonathan Coudrill, a local folk singing character who collected old Rolls, Allards and so forth. Stephen and five of the others clubbed together to form a syndicate, with shares and voting rights, and bought the Essex for, I think, £20. None of them was old enough to have a driving licence, so they got Jonathan to drive the car out of St Ives to the home of one of the boys' parents, Maimie Hardy, who lived on the slope of Trencrom – and more important, owned a fairly large field. Here, away from the legal confinements of the public highway, the boys really enjoyed themselves, driving round and round a measured track and generally having great fun. This was just as well as it was the most they were ever to get out of what I personally regarded a something of a mechanical monument ... and after a year or so of incredibly desultory usage, the car ended in a local car dump.

There were other joint ventures of a similar nature – motor cycles, sailing dinghies and so forth. But the pre-eminent central focus, for several years, to return to my story, was to be Stephen's Attic. As time went by its decor and contents became more and more bizarre. I often used to take a peep and wonder, nervously, what the local council, or the police, might have had to say. On one occasion I found draped around the walls several appropriated local road signs – Virgin Street, Court Cocking, Salubrious Place – plus one or two striking religious posters of the Jehovah's Witness variety: *Prepare to Meet Thy God;* from a more functional point of view Stephen had laboriously created in one corner a tiny 'Coke' bar, the surface rather puzzlingly entirely covered with old tin caps of bottles – a touch I only fully appreciated when I accidentally put my hand and received a mild electric shock.

Apparently being of a suspicious nature Stephen had devised this form of protection against any attempt to procure bottles of coke without payment. For, oh, yes, payment was involved in Stephen's Club (though we had no idea for a long time, and would not really have approved). It's true that some of the payment may have offset expenses (though with electricity coming off my bill and the cokes paid for separately anyway it was a little difficult to think what these expenses might have been). However, I can't help thinking the profit motive – which in much later adult days Stephen was to attack so vehemently – came into the picture quite a lot. Especially as later on we discovered that Stephen had built up quite a lucrative side-line of letting off the loft recess, each equipped with an old but no doubt comfortable mattress, to various boys for a necking session with their respective girl friends. No doubt with a few candles in bottles providing the only vague illumination everything was very romantic.

One of the dubious attractions about Stephen's Attic Club was that access was extremely difficult, not to say hazardous. For a long time indeed, the only way up was to enter the upstairs lavatory and then climb a single rickety ladder through a hole up in the roof. A procedure complicated enough, and sometimes actually embarrassing on the return journey should the lavatory be occupied. In the end we managed to get a local carpenter to build a small trap-door off the landing, but the approach was always in the form of a ladder, and it would have taken any unexpected caller quite a few minutes to reach the attic – by which time (as I know happened on one or two alarming occasions) the road signs and any other incriminating evidence could no doubt be whipped away.

Jess and I would often catch a strangely harmonious sound wafting through the long corridors of St Christopher's to where we sat in our own little private room looking over Porthmeor. Intrigued, we would move along to stand under the swaying humming loft above our heads. The noise would in fact be the sound of a couple of dozen teenagers, including Stephen, Demelza and Genevieve, singing some of the current folk songs. While there might be no Joan Baez or Pete Seeger among them, the effect of their fresh young voices raised up lustily against the accompaniment of a couple of guitars played by Stephen and his friend Paul Richards, was often quite poignant. Listening to them singing 'All my tomorrows' and 'We shall Overcome,' Jess and I would offer up a silent prayer for the curiously innocent and courageous young of today.

Not everyone who called at St Christopher's was Stephen's friend, of course – though often it seemed that most of them were: Each of the children acquired their own friends. At that time Gill was passing very much through a boyfriend period. It was through her that we had one of our most unexpected guests, a Gallic one – Jean-François, a name etched into the family history. It came about like this. Gill was studying for her GCE and it seemed to us it would be an excellent plan for her to spend a holiday in France and really get to know the language. Money being limited we explored the popular system of exchange holidays. Through a London agency we established contact with a French family in Paris who wished their son to spend a holiday in England, and quite quickly matters were arranged. As it happened in the end Gill went for her holiday first and was back home after a delightful month, spent largely at an old château, before the final arrival of Jean-François.

Eagerly we asked her what our visitor was like. Gill gave an enigmatic smile. 'Well, he isn't quite what you expect perhaps.'

A day or two later we understood exactly what she meant. In some vague way I must have expected a fresh-faced schoolboy; after all he *was* aonly about fifteen years old, not much older than Gill.

Jean-François, alas, was very different; certainly the oldest and most adult fifteen-year-old we had ever met. Although not very tall he nevertheless had all the natural attributes of adulthood, not only in the way he dressed but in the way he thought, walked and – well, behaved. Within a short time of arriving Jean-François was discoursing with aplomb about French politics, Algeria, the last war, literature, almost anything under the sun – and when I say with aplomb I do not mean foolishly; for a fifteen-year-old he was extremely intelligent, much more worldly than most English boys of that age. But all the same there was really, it soon became apparent, only one subject that interested him.

'Gillian,' said Jean-François, after allowing a suitable time to pass for the niceties of settling in. 'You would like to go to the flics, yes?' A wink, a raising of the eyebrows, and then what we came to recognise as a standard Jean-François ploy – finger between lips and a flick to express a loud and somehow curiously suggestive 'Pouff!'

Flattered no doubt, Gillian departed, returning later that evening rather pink and slightly dishevelled.

'Where's Jean-François?' we said anxiously. 'Supposing he gets lost?'

'Huh!' snorted Gill with feeling. 'Don't worry – he can look after himself.'

She went to bed still flushed and bright-eyed – Jean-François returned, whistling loudly, about an hour later.

'Are you all right, Jean-François?'

'Oh, yes, yes.' Wink, eyebrows, pouff. 'Yes – I just take ze look at ze sights of St Ives, yes?' Eyebrows. 'Not bad, eh?'

During the next few days Jean-François concentrated not only on seeing but getting to know the sights of St Ives. From our point of view he was certainly little trouble to entertain. After a morning cup of coffee he would saunter off down to the harbour to bask in the sunshine and see what was doing. Sometimes he would return for lunch, but more often he would be off on some ambitious exploits to escort pretty nineteen-year-old girls to Clodgy Point, or maybe even further. In summer time the girls of St Ives emerge at their prettiest in their new dresses and a Gallic charmer was in his element.

Now and then we would attempt to fulfil our duties as exchange hosts.

'Jean-François, how would you like to take a trip to Falmouth today? We might take you on the ferry boat to St Mawes. Very interesting.'

At this Jean-François's face would screw up in an agony of superficial regret, and he would spread his hands out hopelessly.

'What a pity – I have ze date with Margaret. It would be, how you say, ungallant not to meet her, yes?'

Margaret one day, Phyllis the next, Jean the next – we began to wonder ... and worry ... and wonder. After all we were responsible for Jean-François. We didn't want him to come to any moral harm while in our care.

'Don't worry,' snorted Gillian one day. 'It's the girls of St Ives who need protecting.'

By now, I should explain, Jean-François had taken to talking volubly at all times and thoroughly wearing us out. We began counting anxiously the days to the end of his month's stay. When respite was near we mellowed a little and proposed as a special treat a trip to the Isles of Scilly. Rather to our surprise Jean-François agreed to come. On the way from St Ives to Penzance by car he chattered away incessantly: at the harbour his voice went on and on; as we boarded the *Scillonian* he was in full spate. At last the voyage began, the ship began steaming along in the shelter of West Penwith, and still Jean-François talked and talked ...

Suddenly, half an hour later, when we had passed the Longships lighthouse and were exposed to the full vagaries of the Atlantic, on what can often be an extremely rough crossing, we became conscious of a strange silence. All that could be heard was the hiss of the wind, the squeaking of seagulls, the boom of the waves breaking on the ship's bow.

'Jean-François? Jean-François?'

We found him leaning over the rails at the stern, being very sick. We left him there to recuperate, not altogether displeased at the respite. However, within half an hour he had recovered and what was more had discovered a party of thirty Swedish girls also having a day out to the Scillies. In no time at all he was back in his element, and proceeded to cause consternation on the Island by stopping girls in the street and insisting on dancing the 'twist' with them.

On his last evening we took Jean-François out for a farewell dinner. Progress along the crowded harbour front was rather like a procession of royalty. Every few yards we had to stop to acknowledge a greeting from one pretty piece or another. Each time Jean-François bowed courteously and winked and pouffed. ''Allo, Jean darling.' ''Allo, Mary,' ''Allo, Pat.' And then once or twice a remark that alarmed us considerably. 'Zee you next year, yes?'

In fact we were never to see Jean-François again, much to Gill's relief, at least. She by now had grown older and wiser – though still rather young, we thought, to be about to elope with a young art student, Alan Moss. Since both Jess and I had in our youths behaved in very similar ways there was nothing much we could do about it: all the same Jess felt rather at a loss, and afterwards quite weepy, when one day we found a car outside with Gill and Alan and a friend sitting in it, and were greeted by the announcement 'We're off to Liverpool for the winter.' And off they went ... it might, of course, have just been one of those fleeting romances, but in fact the relationship was to blossom and develop into marriage, and now Gill and Alan have been married for many years.

This was really the period of the beginning of the first break up of the Val Baker family (I use the numerative adjective precisely, for reasons which will become ironically clear in Part Four). Martin had already wended his rather weary way from the friendliness of Falmouth Art School, where he had been sincerely happy, to the scattered environs of Hornsey School of

Art in North London, where it became increasingly obvious he was most unhappy. When it was too late we discovered that Martin had so lost confidence that he was not going into classes but wandering about London, or sitting in his bed-sitter – in the end he could not face the life any longer and left. We were very upset about this, and felt the college should have been more aware of such a state of mind in a pupil, but by then there was nothing much to be done about it – and for the time being Martin disappeared into the limbo of London driving a van for a wine merchant.

Now yet a third member of the family was emigrating – not all that far, to Camborne. This was Jane, who had increasingly come to feel somehow a misfit in the family life, with the result of a series of blazing rows, so that no doubt it was best for all if she had a period away. She took digs in Camborne and became a pupil at the Cornwall Technical College, and soon found a niche for herself there, organizing various social events and making a wide circle of friends.

If it had not been for Stephen's Club and his extraordinarily enormous circle of friends and acquaintances who all seemed to flood our house every evening and the whole of the weekends, we might I suppose have noticed the family break more acutely. As it was, the family life at St Christopher's *appeared* to carry along with unfailing gaiety and good-humoured pandemonium … especially in those marvellous summer months, when there was usually money in the kitty, and surfing all day on the beaches, with perhaps an evening run over to Zennor or Gurnard's Head for a drink or a barbecue … and then finally, too, there was always Christmas-time and our annual Boxing Night Party, for which not only did all the family get together, but also, it often seemed, half of St Ives as well. We had begun those parties in those far off days at St Hilary and kept up the custom ever since, and I must admit there could not be a better setting than our 65 foot long room at St Christopher's, with doors opening out on to the beach and the distant Atlantic waves. We would put candles in bottles down the sides, have a barrel of beer and a huge bowl of hot punch.

At first our friends would trickle in quietly, but as soon as the pubs were closed there would be an absolute avalanche – so much so, in fact, that we used to employ Stephen and his friends to stand at the door keeping a check against too many intruders. In no time it would seem that the long room was bursting to the seams with crowds of people whirling round, or clustering in animated groups. The family would be there in full force, of course, and I am sure that when we all remember those far off days, as like as not we remember those boxing nights, when the punch ran free, the music blared, the cool Atlantic air wafted in the open beach doors, and everyone was happy.

Part Three

The Val Bakers Afloat

I

Cruising Up the Rivers

Ironically it was while we lived in the dusty heart of London, and not along the sea-washed shores of Cornwall, that our family first began its running love affair with boating. I suppose I had always had a sneaking hankering for the life afloat, ever since as a boy I used to cycle up and down the River Thames towpath at Hampton Court, watching the smart cruisers gliding past … and it was to the Thames again that I turned for our first experience of a boating holiday.

On this occasion we rented a 35-foot motor cabin cruiser for an epic journey from Thames Ditton up to Goring on the River Thames. This experience might have been less unnerving had it not been for the presence of Genevieve, still a very small child at that time. The other children were self-propelling and could look after themselves but each time we approached a lock my attention would be diverted by a wild scream from Jess:

'Genevieve's going overboard.'

The first time this happened I whirled around, let go the gear and just in time grabbed Genevieve by her knees as she was about to topple over.

The boat, with a reverberating crash, hit the lock door and bounced back. Within a few seconds the water seeping out of the lock had swung our boat round so that she lay exactly across the entrance, causing what I suppose on the roads would be called a hold-up.

At this stage I became aware of a benevolent, brown-faced weather-beaten man in blue uniform bending over the edge of the lock. As I cowered in fear before the expected wrath, he spoke gently, as to a child, and gave me a few simple instructions about how to use a boat-hook to push the boat round, and then how to tie her up to wait until the lock opened, and so on, *ad infinitum*. Like all the lock-keepers – twenty-three I think there were in all – we encountered during our journey, this one was almost excessively tolerant of behaviour which must have seemed to him bordering on lunacy. As we progressed, and I rammed lock after lock, or at the least got our bow stuck between the white posts that were all that stopped us being swept over a weir, I found that it was never the patient lock-keepers, but rather sniggering groups of children and holiday makers who rubbed salt into the wounds of our hurt pride.

'The fleet's in port!' they would chortle. Or, 'Three cheers for the Admiral!'

And when, as sometimes happened, we ran aground through going too close to the bank, they lined up in rows to watch sardonically while Jess and I and the older children heaved and pushed and rocked the boat in our efforts to get free.

Somehow repetition of these experiences bred in us a sort of hardening, so that we even ceased to feel humiliation. But nothing overcame my allergy to locks. From the moment we sighted one to the moment of nosing our way out, probably knocking some innocent waiting boat into the bank *en route,* my knees were jelly, my heart in my mouth. I could never overcome my lost feeling without a brake to apply. As we glided into the lock my own thought was somehow to lasso one of the bollards (mooring posts to you) with one of the innumerable ropes lying around our decks. As I also had to stay at the wheel, this entailed my shouting wild, peremptory instructions to Martin, already jumpy because he has inherited my expect-the-worst nature, and to Gill – less jumpy, but easily wounded by imputations of inefficiency.

'Throw the ropes! Quick! Jump – jump ashore. Oh you fatheads … !'

So the stream of invective flowed from the petty tyrant that these terrible locks had made me. After three locks Gill would no longer speak to me. After I had replaced her with her mother, one more lock sufficed for a quick marital exchange of views which resulted in Martin and me having to manage the locks for the remainder of the trip.

So we meandered up the river, through lock after lock. No sooner were we free of the tentacles of one than something in the very air warned me of the impending horror of another. Penton Hook, Bell Weir, Old Windsor, Romney, Temple, Hambledon, Boulter's, Sonning, Mapledurham – they often had delightful names, matching their pretty gardens and romantic surroundings. For Jess and the other children, reclining lazily on the cabin roofs, they represented part of a pageant of quiet English beauty ... but for Martin and me they represented minor nightmares, filled with bollards and warps, ropes and fend-offs, sudden alarming ascents or descents which invariably found the boat floating out into the middle, necessitating one or other of us making a wild, quite dangerous leap from the shore on to the boat.

And then there was always Genevieve. By some demonic instinct, she indulged in the full flower of wickedness at lock-times. If she was in the cabin, her blonde head would be thrust out of a port-hole, thus to be in immediate danger of being crushed against the lock walls. If put in the cockpit, within $9\frac{1}{2}$ seconds (yes, I timed her) she would have climbed over the side to get into the water. And if taken on the cabin roof ...

The wonder of it is that I survived at all. What's more, though but dimly, I seem to recollect moments of pleasure – between locks, of course. The green beauty of meadows at Cookham, the old world charm of Marlow, the faint thrill of coming up Henley Regatta course, the incredibly lovely Medmenham Abbey, Hambledon Lock and its frothing weir ...

After our experience on the Thames we were naturally eager to try fresh waters. After many pleasant winter evenings spent pouring over catalogues and guide books, we eventually decided to try the Norfolk Broads. Nothing more opposite to Cornwall than Norfolk could be imagined, which is probably why we enjoyed the holiday so much. Needless to say any holiday for a family of eight is something like a military operation. (Sometimes I think that perhaps our real reason for settling in Cornwall is that living in such an ideal holiday centre obviates the necessity for embarking on official holidays). All the same, we do crave for a change sometimes, and Norfolk certainly provided it.

First we had to make all the preparations beforehand, and fortunately the Broads are so highly organised that there is almost an embarrassment of choices, especially early in the season. We plumped for the first week in May and put our deposit down on just about the biggest motor cruiser in the entire Norfolk Broads Fleet, one of the Admirable 8-berths boats based on Browns Boatyard at Brundall, near Norwich.

It was exciting to get all the publicity material and tick off the list of the boat's accessories, and browse through some of the other Broads literature. We bought coloured maps outlining the whole area of the Broads and planned our routes as far as was possible. Hitherto I had always conceived a vague idea of the Broads as a gathering of lakes: now it became obvious that they consisted really of several interlocking rivers, and that in fact our trip would involve quite long distances.

Still the longest distance of all would be getting from St Ives, Cornwall, to Norwich, in all a distance of nearly 400 miles. At that time we were running one of the oldest and most decrepit cars I have ever owned, a 1935 14-horse power Rover saloon which I had bought on the spur of the moment for £14 at a Hayle garage. It looked an absolute wreck, the bodywork rusted, the mudguards rattling, and the fact that the body was very low on the ground added to a general air of being in the last stages of consumption. But in fact – as I had found with a previous Rover, a 1927 coupé – it had a heart of gold, or I should say an engine that would chug on undaunted forever. For a car of its kind it was surprisingly fast, too, and we always enjoyed zooming past more modern cars and watching their amazed looks. The main thing was that for all its woebegone appearance I knew the Rover was reliable and would get us to Norwich or anywhere else for that matter. Four hundred miles in a day, though, with a family of eight aboard, all squashed together, did not appeal to any of us.

In the end we compromised by heading for Cambridge, where Jess's brother-in-law was vicar of St George's Church, and also sent Stephen and Jane by train, to lighten the load. We had another reason for sending two of the children by train; they were thus able to deliver a large box of pottery to a London shop we supply. Whenever we sent pottery by rail or road we were always getting complaints of breakages, so this time we went to enormous lengths to guarantee personal door-to-door service. Our friend Anthony Richards drove the two children and their box to St Erth station; from there they travelled on the train to Paddington, where they were met by two other friends, Susan and Ricky Richard, who drove them direct to the pottery shop. It would have seemed impossible for anything to go wrong and we were therefore astounded when the pottery shop sorrowfully reported a large number of breakages. Jane and Stephen swore black and blue that they had been careful ... and then it came out. At St Erth a 'nice porter' insisted on carrying the box for them – and half way along dropped it on the platform!

In the end we managed our marathon journey without hitch and after leaving St Ives at nine o'clock, drove into Cambridge at half past seven. The next day we drove the comparatively short 60 miles over to Norwich, and pulled in at the boatyard about three o'clock feeling stirrings of familiar excitement. Almost immediately the children spotted our boat and gave whoops of delight – and I must say not without justification. *Admiral Three* really was a handsome craft, a long streamlined motor cruiser 42 feet in length with well fitted cabins – in all I think there were five cabins, one of them being the sitting room by day. Jess and I even had the luxury of a double bed in ours! Cooking was done in comfort by a bottle-gas cooker, there was running water from big tanks which we were able to fill up easily, and a profusion of household equipment. Altogether we were highly pleased, and after the mechanic had taken us for a short run to brush up my previous experience with a cruiser on the Thames, we set off on our week's voyage.

At least, I thought, this time we haven't got the problem of the locks which alarmed us a good deal on the Thames. However, we soon found one or two other hazards – one of the most insidious being that the Yare, the Waveny, the Bure, the Thurne and the Ant, the main rivers making up the Broads, are tidal rivers. You are likely, as we did, to moor for the night at some pleasant spot, your mooring ropes hanging languid and loose from the posts, and wake up in the morning in alarm to find the boat heeling over and the ropes taut and fully stretched – all because you had forgotten the tide would go down six feet or so during the night! We found this situation *in extremis* once near Oulton Broad when we came round a bend and found the extraordinary spectacle of a large motor-cruiser right up on a bank, with only the stern dangling in the water, and her occupants waving pitifully for help. It appeared they had somehow got the nose ashore when the tide was high and left it like that. In the end it required the efforts of ourselves and two other boats to tow them back into the water.

Not only was the *Admiral* a much larger cruiser than the one we had taken up the Thames but we also had the extra treat of a 14-foot sailing dinghy, which we towed along at the back when not in use. For a visit to the Broads a shallow-bottomed boat like a dinghy is essential, for the real delight of the Broads is explorations up narrow creeks and broads (or small lakes). Our dinghy had a gay red sail and provided the older children with an unfailing source of separate enjoyment. I can't say we were sorry, for it meant a bit of peace for us. Our two youngest, Demelza and Genevieve, then aged nine and six respectively, were rightly too nervous of entrusting themselves in the sailing dinghy to the hazardous care of the older children. But Martin, Gill, Jane and Stephen spent hours in the dinghy tacking from side to side of the river, or disappearing down some enormous Broad.

Our friend Patrick Wyld had lent us a very efficient Swiss cine-camera and we used quite a bit of film shooting the older children at play in their sailing dinghy. On one occasion we decided on a definite sequence; they would sail a certain distance and then start fishing. Jess filmed the journey and then sat patiently waiting, in focus, while the fishing line was dangled up and down. At last there were shrieks and yells and Martin pulled up a line on which dangled the smallest, most attractive fish I have ever seen. While Jess whirred away on the camera there seemed to be a sudden crisis in the boat, much argument and gesticulation – in the end, to our astonishment, the fish was thrown back into the water. It transpired that the hook had got stuck in its gullet and after frantically trying to remove it the children felt pity and put the fish back.

Among some other excellent film 'material' provided during the course of our trip was an occasion when we were all sitting down to an evening meal, having moored in a beautiful isolated bank somewhere near Barton Broad. Suddenly the boat rocked violently from side to side and we all went sprawling. Rushing on deck we found two mournful-eyed brown carthorses nuzzling at the portholes. When we appeared they took fright a little and lumbered down the footpath, but after a while we calmed them down. Then, greatly daring, Demelza and Genevieve, tip-toed along the towpath towards the horses, holding out lumps of sugar. In their mixture of daring and reticence, cheek and nervousness, somehow was epitomised the whole story of childhood.

Although there are no locks on the Broads there are, as I say, other hazards, among them the frequent possibility of running aground too near the banks or of being unable to turn the huge boat round after having penetrated some steadily narrowing creek. On the River Yare, leading from Yarmouth up to Norwich, there was also the alarming possibility of rounding a bend and finding oneself almost bow to bow with a bulky cargo steamer from Rotterdam or Hamburg. We have several beautiful shots of one of these huge tankers gliding peacefully through the smooth river water – taken just before its enormous wash nearly swept us into the bank. Perhaps the most nerve-racking experience of all was the successful mooring of the boat for the night. After all, *Admiral Three* was 42 feet long, and took quite a bit of manipulation, especially when it was a case of nosing in between a buried tree trunk and a protruding bank, or stopping dead in the only 42 foot length of water of any depth.

I have to admit that I found the strain of this, the enormous heavy responsibility of being captain and responsible for seven other lives, a bit wearing. At any rate I was quickly nicknamed by the rest of the family 'Mr Panic.' 'Look out,' they would call out, as soon as some crisis loomed, 'here comes Mr Panic.' I felt this was often a little hard as it was I who had to take the blame if we ran into a sailing boat or went aground. All the same I can see in retrospect that the effect of responsibility did make me extra touchy.

This was reflected amusingly in the one and only time I was allowed out in the sailing boat. Although brave enough at surfing in high seas I always feel uneasy about deep water, though willy-nilly I have learned to swim a few strokes. There is something about the dark sinister depths of mid-river that certainly does not put me at ease. So, when we set off in the dingy and the wind began to heel her over, I clutched the sides grimly and probably looked as if I was praying for safety – which I was. I was certainly in favour of being cautious, and since my companions were Stephen, whose life has been one reckless escapade after another, and Gill, who is quick-witted and efficient at most things she does, my pitiful efforts to be a good sailing companion were not appreciated. In fact after we had done one round of Barton Broad the red dinghy was brought up smartly alongside her mother ship and the captain was pointedly asked to disembark.

On another occasion I felt that my caution had been justified. By then we had reached our further point on the journey, having travelled down the River Yare and across Breydon Water and then up the Bure as far as Wroxham. Known as 'the Queen of the Broads,' Wroxham is a mile long and half a mile wide and, covering a total area of 120 acres, it makes a fine spot for sailing. On the day we paid our visit there was quite a small gale blowing which is all right for experienced sailors, not so promising for novices. Nevertheless Jess chose this occasion to try her hand at sailing, and with Stephen and Jane for companions set off across the wide broad. I decided to film this interesting debut, and had several good shots of the little red yacht fairly skimming across the water. Then – pardonably, since it was heading at great speed for the opposite bank – Jess must have decided to turn, or 'bring her round' as I think yachting parlance has it.

I was so engaged in keeping the camera in focus that for a few seconds I did not really take in what was happening. Then there were yelps of impending disaster from the boat, and of foreboding from *Admiral Three* – as the little sailing dinghy heeled right over on her side. I am not exaggerating when I say at one moment she was at complete right angles to the water and her occupants appeared about to be thrown in. However, by some miracle she tipped back, though only partly, and we could see that they were all a little shaken. This it appeared was a case for rescue, so we pulled in our anchor quickly, started the diesel, and roared our way across to pick up the little dinghy. 'Mr Panic' was indeed relieved when finally all were aboard again.

Not all our time on the Broads was spent on the water, or in such antics, of course. We were constantly pulling in at some picturesque spot for happy-go-lucky exploration of the surrounding countryside. Some of the smaller broads, like Rockland and the two Salhouse Broads, were really delightful, quite wild and unspoiled. Contrariwise, there was a picturesque attraction about some of the Broadland villages, even the rather luxurious ones like Horning. It was easy to envy the residents living in beautiful old houses with smooth gracious lawns sloping down to the river's edge, and a smart motor launch waiting at their beck and call. We couldn't help being amused, on reaching Wroxham, to find many similarities with St Ives, for here is the capital of Broadland, complete with many gift shops and tea-shops. Apparently it was from Wroxham that the whole idea of the Norfolk Broads as a holiday centre originated. More than 70 years ago, to quote the official guide book, 'an adventurous Norwich man and two companions trundled a tiny boat on a wheelbarrow to Wroxham Bridge and set out on a momentous voyage of discovery.' The Broads had only been vaguely known but the stories told by the three men in a boat soon set people clamouring for an opportunity to cruise the unique waterways. A small boatyard was established at Wroxham Bridge about 1880 and then came more and more yards until now boat letting has developed into a big industry.

There is a wealth of information about how to travel up and down the Broads so that it would seem difficult to go wrong. All the same we managed to do so when we ventured up the River Thurne towards Hickling Broad and Horsey Mere. We were looking forward to this part of the trip as Hickling is one of the largest of all the Broads and Horsey is very beautiful.

Alas, as we hummed our way up the Thurne and rounded a bend we came upon an alarming sight – Potter Heigham

Bridge. This is very old, very small, very humped – and very low. So low, in fact that it became pretty obvious that the 42 foot long, 7 foot high Admiral motor cruiser just wasn't going to scrape underneath. We consulted local experts and while one or two said if we waited until the very lowest point of the ebb tide we might just make it the consensus was against.

So, regretfully, we turned round and resumed what was now the homeward part of our journey. This meant a second trip via Yarmouth, but this time we were not going to make the dreadful mistake of our outgoing trip and stop for a look at this well-known seaside town. Perhaps it was the contrast with all the pretty countryside we had been passing through, but as we trailed with the children along the squalid commercialised front at Yarmouth, every other shop a bingo hall or an amusement arcade, everywhere a faded tired decaying air, our spirits really drooped. Never was the whole family gladder to get back on board the *Admiral* and open full throttle up river again.

Our homeward journey took us through two of the biggest stretches on the Broads; these were Breydon Water, the remnant of a vast stretch of estuary of the North Sea that once extended to Norwich and Beccles but is now silting up (a rather forlorn and lonely stretch of four miles with only one narrow channel for safe navigation) and Oulton Broad, just outside Lowestoft. At Oulton, obviously, were gathered some of the élite of Broads' yachtsmen, and this is also where some of Britain's crack outboard motor boat races are held. We found a large yacht station and many useful amenities, and our children embarked riotously on games on a handy playground. However what we remember Oulton for more than anything else is that it is the spot where the children's macintoshes went over-board. I can't quite remember how it happened, but we were just in the middle of trying to make the stylish getaway from the yacht basin obviously expected of an Admiral cruiser when there were sudden shouts and screams … looking round I found three separate children's macintoshes floating in three separate parts of Oulton Broad. It was mid-day, a busy time on the Broad, yachts were criss-crossing, motor cruisers coming in to berth, small boys fooling about in dinghies – not the happiest of times in which to start manoeuvring in a 42-foot ocean liner, as it seemed just then, to pick up children's waterlogged macintoshes. Grimly I kept reversing and turning and going forward and reversing and – well, in the end Martin jumped into the dinghy and rescued one mac, while Gill, leaning over the edge of the *Admiral* with a boat hook, hooked up the other two. Then, rather shamefacedly, I swung the wheel round and headed *Admiral* very firmly for the Haddiscoe New Cut and Reedham and the River Yare and back to Brundall.

*

When we came to look back upon it the Norfolk Broads holiday was voted an all round success, and the three colour films we had taken proved to be a delightful memoir. In fact, we were spurred on by this successful venture to explore new waterways.

For our next waterways holiday we would try a canal we decided. We sat poring over the map, embarrassed by a profusion of choices. Of course, we realised that some canals passed through industrial cities and though possibly interesting, were hardly to be recommended for an annual family cruise. We hesitated for a long time over the Oxford Canal, which looked delightful and ended up near Stratford-on-Avon. But then our eyes were caught by some interesting wriggling red lines on the left of the map, and the magic words 'Shropshire Union Canal' – and then the even more magical word, Wales (for both Jess and I are Welsh, and are forever feeling the call back there). Yes, this was it, without a doubt. We would travel down the Shropshire Union Canal to where it branched off into the narrow Llangollen Canal and then we would make a trip right through the heart of the Welsh hill country.

One again such a trip involved some mammoth planning: once again we were fortunate to find another relative of Jess's, sister Marjorie, prepared to put up a family of eight en route for the canals. We had indeed contemplated beginning our journey from Wolverhampton but I jibbed when I worked out there would be 43 locks even before we reached the Llangollen Canal, and instead we had booked with a firm at Chester. This meant that in all we had an even longer journey than the previous year. In the meantime we had finally packed up the old Rover, not through any real fault but I'm afraid for love of another lady.

At a village called Angarrack near Hayle, there is quite a local character called Jack Collinson. He is a car dealer with a great gift of the gab and also a genuine love for vintage and veteran cars, indeed his name is well known all over the country in that field. I had in fact bought the old Rover from him, and now, hearing that he had moved into an old country house at Angarrack, I was tempted one afternoon to pay him a visit. It was a fascinating afternoon. Scattered around the grounds of this rambling old house were dozens of old cars, the more precious of them tucked away in stables and garages. Enjoying himself in showing us round Jack Collinson would suddenly fling open a door and announce proudly: 'Bull Nose Morris, 1925 – Look at her condition.' Or 'Austin Laundalette, 1928, spotless!' And so they were – they were vintage cars which he had picked up all over the country and brought home to work on. Quite probably he would give seven coats of paint to some of them as part of the process of restoring them to their original condition. One of his prides and joy was 'Daisy,' an original Austin Chummy saloon, about 1927, absolutely bright and shiny as new. There was a price of £500 on her, but that was simply, I guessed, to scare buyers off. Some months later we were at a Traction Rally near Redruth and there was Jack Collinson himself proudly driving 'Daisy' in a parade of vintage cars.

We had not been there half an hour when we both fell in love with the magnificent old Austin Laundalette, very high up and old-fashioned, with a luxurious interior of the sort associated with royalty. The history of the car was that it had belonged for many years to a well known writer with a large family who each summer used to drive himself and his children all the way down to the South of France. We could hardly be blamed for indulging in wishful thinking of repeating this operation; but the price of £200 was beyond our means. However, tucked away in another shed, we found recompense in the shape of another early (1933) Austin tourer which, though rather dirty and generally needing doing up, was in serviceable mechanical order. What was more to the point it was going for £40. We had a trial run in her and then took the plunge. We spent a bit more money on getting her into really good condition, the main item being an attractive new red hood, and then she was ready for service again.

So this was the car in which we were to set out for our holiday on the Llangollen Canal. If ever I have had any doubts about the reliability of good old cars – by which I mean old cars that have been well looked after – then our experience with Josephine, as we nick-named our tourer, put an end to them. We had been given confidence, anyway, firstly by our friend Dennis Cotterell of the St Erth Garage, whose own twin loves are steam-engines and old cars (he had had his eye, we learned later, on this one), and then by old Mr Tregarthern, head of a Penzance firm of motor car hood-makers. It was a pleasure to see the way the old craftsman walked round the car and ran his hand lovingly over the familiar pre-war Austin lines. He delivered a brief but biting homily on the respective quality of the materials of old and modern cars and then promised to make a good job of a new hood – which indeed he did.

As the week for our holiday drew nearer we all became very excited, and none more than Demelza, whose imagination always tended to soar away. Alas, at just this time Demelza was attacked by a very unimaginary trouble. Three days before we were due to go to Chester she went down with a high temperature and vomiting and all the other symptoms of one of the inevitable childhood ailments. In the end in the middle of the night we had to get a doctor, it was so alarming, and later that day she had to be taken off to St Michael's Hospital, Hayle, where after examination it was decided that she had some infection which would take quite a while to clear up. The doctor made it quite clear to us that there was no chance whatsoever of her coming on a long trip such as we planned –

indeed she would need to stay in hospital at least ten days.

Suddenly we were faced with one of those agonising quandaries which parents of large families are always half prepared for – but which in our case has mercifully rarely happened. I was very tempted myself to try and re-arrange the trip, postpone it a week or a fortnight, but this would have been very complicated, and there was no guarantee that Demelza would have been able to come even then. The doctor said it would be a pity to spoil the holiday for all the others, and as Demelza had been in St Michael's once before and seemed to like the nuns there very much, reluctantly we decided that we would have to take our holiday without her. Fortunately she was too low at the time to really appreciate what was happening, but towards the end of the week she became much better and we then received two or three heart-rending letters written from her lonely hospital bed.

Not unnaturally when finally we called to collect her after the holiday I approached the hospital in some fear and trembling, expecting to find a tearful wistful-looking child. Instead we were greeted by a bouncing happy little girl who was 'in' with all the sisters and nuns, and had learned from one of them to play the piano and seemed to have had a really good time in her own way.

As it was, our drive up north went like clockwork – until we reached Wolverhampton and then kept getting lost trying to find my sister-in-law's house. As before a couple of the children had gone by a different route to lighten the load, this time Martin and Gill, both of whom had recently entered their beatnik phase. When we finally drove up in the evening we found Marjorie and her husband Jim still trying to recover from the shock of greeting a jeaned and jerseyed Martin, most of his face obliterated by waving blond hair and an enormous rucksack humped on one shoulder. This, by the way, following the earlier arrival of winkle-pickered Gill also complete with body-fitting jeans, a boy friend's sweater and the most heavily mascaraed eyes to have appeared in Wolverhampton for some time. Still, joking apart, we were all very thankful to spend a comfortable night after such a long journey, and the next day

Marge and Jim drove in their car to take some of our load and came to see us off at Chester.

Owing to the fact that canals naturally impose limitations on the size of craft that use them we had decided on this occasion to split our party and hire two four-berth motor cruisers. I was rather against this, clinging to the idea of family unity, but Jess, with bitter memories of preparing huge meals for eight, was sternly for, and in retrospect I had to admit she was probably right. So now, when we got to the boatyard, Martin, Gill, Jane and Stephen eagerly boarded their craft, *Bobby,* while Jess and I with little Genevieve, and a sad thought for Demelza four hundred miles away in St Michael's Hospital, boarded the other one, *Beryl.* At least we spent about two hours transferring an enormous amount of material from Josephine (funny how feminine cars and boats appear to be) to the boats. There was more than usual because, whereas last year we had had the food delivered locally in advance to the boat, this year we were working to a pretty tight budget and had brought most of our food with us from stocks. Furthermore Jess had worked out a rough figure of £1 a day for each boat, and we had given their first week's money to Martin and Gill with the instructions that they would have to manage on that.

At last all seemed ready and I went into the boatyard office to settle up – to be greeted by a real body-blow. After taking the precaution of pocketing the rest of my payment first the manager explained, almost casually, 'By the way, I'm afraid I've got some bad news for you. There's a burst in the canal above Bettisfield – they rang through from Hurlestone Lock this morning.'

'A burst?' I repeated the words uneasily, sensing something disastrous.

'Yes. They won't do anything over the week-end, of course, but the Waterways men will start plugging it on Monday.' He eyed me thoughtfully. 'They say it should be done by the end of the week.'

'But – ?' In my mind I tried to grapple with impossible visions of what happened when canal banks burst. Wouldn't there be a flood? Wouldn't the water pour out for ever and ever? Or what did happen?

It was simple – and disastrous – enough. If a bank burst then the whole amount of water between the two locks would be lost – but by closing the locks at either end any further seepage would be slowed down. However, pretty obviously, if there was no water between two locks then no boat was going to pass that way, unless it was carried by hand.

And alas, I knew, returning to survey our two motor boats with some dismay, not even the Val Baker family could manage that.

When I had consulted the detailed maps which we had obtained from British Waterways I cheered up a little. The break was certainly before the most beautiful and exciting part of the Llangollen Canal – Chirk Aqueduct and Pontcysyllte Aqueduct, one of Thomas Telford's masterpieces – but at least we could spend three days travelling before we reached the break. And then there was always the possibility of a miracle and the break being mended sooner than we thought.

Trying to cheer myself and the family up on these lines I gave the order to set sail, or rather start motors – and off we went. Almost at once we discovered one of many aspects of the canal boats which compared rather unfavourably with the ones we had had on the Broads and the River Thames – the motors were very low powered and we seemed unable to do much more than crawl along at walking speed. In this fashion our little procession chugged away along a long curving bend that took us out of sight of the boat yard and then – crunch, shake, shudder. We, the leading boat, were aground. This was our first experience of many times of going aground, which on the smaller canals is hardly to be avoided, since they are not very deeply dredged except in the very centre.

On this first occasion the 'Mr Panic' in me returned. Fearing we might be stuck there for hours and thus waste valuable time, I sent Stephen running back along the towpath to fetch help from the boatyard, which was still within reach. Eventually a small boat came up and two mechanics got out and tried to free the boat by reversing and going forward: in the end one of them donned waders and got into the river and physically hauled the boat free.

At last we were on our way again. This time I took good care to keep in the middle of the canal, and following closely the first of our two booklets – *Cruising on the Shropshire Union Canal, Ellesmere Port to Autherly Junction* – I led our companion boat under Bridges 119 to 109 as far as where the curving canal came round to the lee of that great eye-catcher, Beeston Castle (first begun in 1220). In the end Beeston Castle became something of a joke to the others because I was very keen to pay a visit of inspection. After spending our first night moored by Bates Mill Bridge, near the Old Shady Inn, I had everyone up early the next morning and walking in beautiful sunshine along the two miles round to the Castle entrance. Alas, when we got there it was to find that it was at present closed on Sundays, though it would be open the week after we had gone away again. Not to be deterred I carefully made a note of the week-day opening times and secretly planned to make a call there on the way back – only in the end to arrive half an hour after closing time.

As it happened so far we had not had to go through a single lock, but after Bates Mill we came to the first of many, Wharton Lock. When we travelled up the Thames the locks worried us, but more as approaching obstacles than for any other reason. The Thames locks are mostly manned by highly efficient lock-keepers and we left all the moving around to them. On the canals it is very different; with the exception of a few junction locks, the locks are un-manned, which means that if you want to take your boat through then you operate the locks yourself.

On the main Shropshire Canal this proved quite arduous work for each lock had double gates. We had been provided with special ratchets for turning the lock gates – perpetual nightmare cry of the trip was 'Where's the ratchet – you've lost our ratchet' – and as soon as we reached a lock gate, if it was shut then two of us ran ahead and began furiously turning the ratchets to either raise or lower the gates. If we were going up river, as in this case, then our job first was to get the inside of the lock to the same level as our stretch of water, when we could open the lower gates and enter; then shut the lower gates and open the far gates, which let water in until we had been raised to the level of the far level of water. I don't know if this makes sense but it is very much the fact of the matter.

Things were much more pleasant all round once we reached Hurlestone Junction where, beside the huge 93 million gallon reservoir which feeds the canal system, the Waterways operate a special four-lock system, each with an independent chamber separated by a short pound. In the guide book it states 'the lower gates of these locks are in two mitreing leaves, while the upper end is closed by a single clapping-gate' – the sort of technical jargon which, sitting at home in the winter, had quite frightened me. However when it came to it everything was perfectly straightforward and there was a real character of a lock-keeper, and his wife, whom we enjoyed chatting to. They lived at a pleasant house at the top of the four locks, looking out for thirty or forty miles over the flat Cheshire countryside below. I was very impressed with this setting, the fact that there were children playing around everywhere, the air of being far from all the stupidity of industrial life (though in fact the great railway centre of Crewe was only 7 miles away). The lock-keeper was a strong and interesting character, and his wife, too. I liked their independent air and warm relationship. It was one of those moments, as I saw them together – which quite often happens to me thank goodness – when I knew at once that here was material for a story. Eventually I wrote it, though not being what is called a commercial one it has not yet sold.

At first the Hurlestone lock-keeper was very dubious about us continuing on our way, pointing out that the level of the water further up had sunk two or three inches and there was no news of the break having been mended. There were already about a dozen boats stranded above the break he said. However in the end he agreed that if we were careful we could probably get at least up to Grindley Brook Staircase Locks, a set of six step-up locks. So with friendly waves we set off along the placid water towards Swanley and Baddiley and Wrenbury.

For the next few miles with the two boats chugging along steadily along lazy winding bends in the narrow peaceful canal we had a taste of one of the most attractive sides of canal life – complete peace and solitude. Later, when we went back and ventured along the Shropshire Union past Nantwich we had a taste of the more commercial side of canal life. I shan't easily forget my embarrassment when I turned our boat behind one of the long British Waterways 'narrow boats,' thinking him safely past – and found to my horror that they were pulling a second boat on a long rope and I was caught on the rope! There traffic was busy with boats of various sizes coming and going on the run from Chester down to Wolverhampton (via the fifteen Audlem Locks, said to be the hardest way of getting out of Cheshire). But here at Wrenbury, where we moored for our second night, under a canopy of waving trees, everything was still and quiet, save for the occasional call of a curlew. We cooked our respective meals and then, as the light was fading, Jess and I took Genevieve for a last walk along the canal bank ahead of us. By the time we turned to come back the stars were peeping in the sky ... and it was most restful and a cheerful sight to see the little flickering lights of the two boats waiting for us. I must say we all slept like logs during the trip, an experience we had found on the Broads as well.

The next day we reached Grindley Brook and a bald notice stating 'No Craft Beyond Here.' This I felt was an occasion for brilliant compromise. Although we had travelled a long way via the canal we were still only about 20 miles from the boatyard we had started from. I got a bus from Whitchurch to Chester, got out our beloved Josephine and drove back to Grindley Brook.

'Not to worry. First thing in the morning we'll all pack into the car and drive to Llangollen – at least we'll see our journey's end even if we can't get all the way by canal.'

And that is just what we did. It was a beautiful sunny day and for the first time since we had the car we were able to have the hood down. As we drove along, Jess and Genny and I in the front, Martin, Gill, Jane and Stephen in the back, hair blown wild by the wind but eyes bright with excitement we really savoured the joys of old-fashioned motoring.

My only regret en route was that we never managed to really see Telford's Pontcysyllte Aqueduct, which is 1007 feet in length and spans the Dee Valley on eighteen piers. At its highest point when crossing the Dee itself the water in the aqueduct is 121 feet above the river, which must make a wonderful sight. However as we came into Llangollen we were delighted with the magnificent setting of that town, with the Dee glistening and frothing on the rocks below – and the canal visible high up on our right. We parked the car and walked up to the last boat house on the canal, where we found to our amusement that the water was reduced to hardly more than eighteen inches in depth and just a few feet wide – just wide and deep enough to allow a single flat bottomed craft to edge along. In the summer horse-drawn boats take visitors along this last couple of miles of the canal, but we were a little early for these. Anyway we had brought a picnic lunch with us, so we walked along the canal bank enjoying the surrounding mountain views, across Ty-Craig Bridge and past the Chain Bridge Hotel and finally up to the old Valve House at the canal terminus which controls and measures the six and a quarter million gallons of water which flow into the canal each day. It is here, too, that Telford's Horseshoe Falls across the Dee make a striking sight.

At Llangollen we had felt all our old longing for Wales stirring again, and we were a little sad to return to the flat fields of Cheshire. I returned the car to the boatyard but I had already begun planning in my mind, and after we had spent two more days on the canal, travelling back to Hurlestone and then up to Nantwich and then along towards Chester, I decided we might as well have one more day in Wales.

So on the Thursday night we moored not far from the boathouse and in the morning I got the car on the road again and this time we had quite a marathon run, taking the coast road from Chester right out via St Asaph and Colwyn Bay to Llandudno. All my childhood holidays were spent in that area and I fancied I knew what would appeal to the whole family, and fortunately I was right. We caught the vehicular tram up to the top of the Great Orme at Llandudno and had our lunch high up with that wonderful view across to Conway and the mountains, with Anglesey away on the right. Later we got in the car again and drove along the (to me) ever familiar and beloved route, Conway Penmaenmawr, Llanfairfechan, Aber, Bangor – with a quick nip across the Menai Bridge to show the children – and then back via Capel Curig and Bettws-y-Coed and Llangollen again. A long day but one we would remember.

At the time I could not help feeling that perhaps the Llangollen Canal trip had not been so successful as previous ones, but it is surprising how in retrospect one gets a different perspective. Jess, for instance, was always to remember the extraordinary peace and quiet of the week. The children, though sometimes bored with the canal's evenness, remembered the amusement of unexpected encounters – like the time when, thinking ourselves expert at getting two boats through one lock at the same time we managed to catch the second boat on a ledge in the rear of the lock, so that it nosedived at an angle of 45-degrees, while Jane, who was sitting inside, issued piercing shrieks.

I think it is the continual operation of the locks that we all remembered most vividly, though the single ones on the Llangollen Canal were much easier. Perhaps the main thing about this, as about any other water-borne holiday we have experienced, was that you really did get away from it all. There was no time, when negotiating locks or river bends with a boatload of children, to think about anything else – no time even to worry about anything except the immediate urgent problem of keeping afloat!

II

A Boat of Our Own

I suppose it was only natural, as our boating adventures and experiences increased, that we should begin to dream of having a boat of our own. Not that we ever expected the dream to materialise – and when it did, there was a sad undertone. What happened was that my mother died and left me a lump sum which perhaps I should have saved for the proverbial rainy day … instead I blued the whole lot on buying our very first boat. True to style in our family, she wasn't just an ordinary boat, either, but a converted MFV (Motor Fishing Vessel), *Sanu,* registered tonnage 23.45, other vital statistics, 60 ft 9 ins length, 18 ft beam, $7\frac{1}{2}$ ft draft … In the bows were two separate cabins, each with two single bunks, next came a larger double cabin with an extra bunk above – opposite that was a smart bathroom with three-quarter size bath and wash basin and calor gas water heater. Next came the saloon with drip feed oil heater and fridge and plenty of cupboard space; adjoining it a very practical galley with sink, gas cooker and more cupboard space. That was the fore-part of the boat; aft there was yet another very large cabin with a double bed and two singles and, tucked behind a curtain, narrow bunks for two more if necessary. Finally, below deck there was a really enormous engine room, so big you could walk round in comfort – the middle dominated by a gleaming Kelvin 88 hp diesel engine that looked well cared for, with a Lister Generator at one side. Even then the layout was not finished – for on deck level there was a handsome wheel house with steering wheel, ship to shore radio, echo sounder, etc., and behind that yet another deck cabin with two comfortable berths. In all, there were five cabins to sleep 13 people, plus a couple of emergency berths if necessary. She was more than a boat, she was a large family house on the water:

From the moment we brought *Sanu* from Southampton down to her permanent mooring at Falmouth that spring our whole way of life seemed to change (I don't know whether to say radically or alarmingly!). For Jess and me there was a new kind of overhanging worry, a niggling anxiety. Was *she* all right? Would the chain hold? Had we shut off the sea cock? What about the calor gas? Were all the portholes closed? I am inclined to worry anyway, and in those early weeks of boat-ownership I think I must have exceeded all previous records. Time after time, especially on a wild and stormy night, I would start awake and think fearfully about my new charge, perhaps rocking violently in the middle of Falmouth Harbour with nothing between her and destruction but a big red mooring buoy and chain. Oh, if only we could have kept her somewhere nice and handy, where we could keep an eye on the poor old thing!

For the children, of course, the change was a more pleasant and exciting one, and they were impatient to celebrate.

'We want to see the boat! When are we going to see the boat?'

After four hectic days at sea with *Sanu* neither Jess nor I minded a brief respite but two days after our return I took pity on the children and we drove them over for, so to speak, a ceremonial introduction. Secretly I was as proud as any father showing off his new infant, so I was naturally flattered when, after we came in view of the harbour and I pointed out *Sanu,* there were gasps of disbelief and astonishment.

'Not *that* one? Why it's the biggest in the harbour.'

This was a slight exaggeration, but all the same *Sanu* was one of the largest, overshadowed only by the large sea-going tugs that moored in rows down the centre lane.

When we had left *Sanu* we had rowed to the pontoon in our Tod dinghy, which was waiting there now for us, bobbing gently in the afternoon swell. Stephen looked momentarily disappointed at seeing no outboard but cheered up when I explained that there was a 15 horse power Gale engine on *Sanu* which as yet we hadn't got around to fitting up on the dinghy.

He clambered excitedly into the front of the dinghy and Jess sat at the back with a slightly more nervous Demelza and Genevieve, and I rowed the family sedately out to their new acquisition.

From the roadway *Sanu* had looked large enough, but now, approaching by dinghy, she looked enormous, like some ocean going liner. I can still remember now the slight feeling of awe that came over me as I looked over my shoulder to make sure I was heading right for the ladder steps which we kept fixed over the side. Was this *really* our boat – our very own?

Once aboard the children ran off on an excited tour of inspection, with Jess and me following more slowly. It was a pleasant occasion, the first time the whole family had been on board together – precursor one vaguely sensed, of so many other times. Jess and I sat on the flat aft cabin rooftop at the back listening to the children's excited cries as they made one discovery after another. One of the unexpected features of *Sanu* was that she was fairly well stocked with all sorts of useful items, such as life-belts, oilskins, flags, caps, torches, lamps, many of which we now unearthed tucked away in cupboard and drawers. More enticing still from the children's point of view there was quite a handsome haul of food stocks put away in the galley for emergencies – though I don't think they were especially attracted to the largest single haul, 17 tins of creamed rice!

Almost as if by instinct the children took over the large aft cabin as their headquarters, which is what Jess and I had in mind anyway. Apart from the saloon this was the largest cabin on the boat and would, in its original version, have been the crew's main sleeping quarters. During our inspection of various other fishing boats I had noted that most of them had this kind of rear quarters. Some indeed had quite extensively planned cabins, with bunks let into the sides in double rows, so providing sleeping accommodation for as many as eight people. Ours was not quite on that scale, but something similar in style – on the right side, or as I now began to remember to call it, the starboard side there was a large double berth, and behind that, that is nearer to the stern, ran a single berth – while on the opposite, port side, there was another single berth. In addition there was room for a diesel oil burning stove, a washbasin, a calor gas water heater and several rows of large cupboards and drawers. The aft cabin was very light and airy, too, for the whole of the centre ran under a large double glass canopy through which Jess and I now peered with amusement watching the scurrying forms of the children. However they soon learned that if they wanted privacy they could easily hang one of the red curtains right across and then indulge in all kinds of secret sessions. On later occasions the aft cabin thus became a gambling saloon, a gang headquarters and something of a necking parlour.

Looking back, the almost excruciating nervousness with which we approached our first few outings in *Sanu* may seem out of proportion; but then one is always alarmed by the unknown. Fortunately over the years Jess and I had taken the precaution of attending navigation classes under Captain Harvey at Penzance, and so I was able to make some sense of the huge Admiralty Charts which now began to accumulate on my desk. I suppose we will never forget our very first outing – all of 18 miles to Mevagissey and back, expecting to sink any moment! After that greatly daring we ventured to Plymouth, and then down to Penzance and Newlyn and even round Land's End to our then home port of St Ives. This latter trip had long been high on our list of priorities, if only because we wished to show *Sanu* off to our friends ... but, of course, whereas most summer evenings St Ives Bay is a calm and beautiful scene, with a cluster of colourful French crabbers anchored in the middle – on the evening we chose, the weather had deteriorated rapidly and we had to spend a miserable night at anchor, tossing and turning, and glad to make for the shelter of Hayle as soon as daylight came.

Still, later the weather relented and we were able to sail over to St Ives making what was later described by one of the fishermen as a 'proper professional' entry. Stephen and his friends jumped ashore with the ropes and soon we were securely tied up and welcoming the harbour master aboard for drinks to mark the occasion.

'Are you sure we'll be all right here?" I asked anxiously, for the last thing I wanted to do was to fall out with the local fishermen.

'Yes, yes, cap'n, you're all right here for the while. And later on, if you're staying we can move you up the quay.'

This in fact was what we did during the odd weeks we spent in St Ives. When we first came in we moored wherever there was a convenient space; then, the next day, perhaps, pulled the boat further up by rope, to get her out of the way of where the larger boats landed their catches.

The period that now ensured was one of forgivable smugness. After all *Sanu* was our boat, and here she lay resplendent and shining in St Ives, for all to see. We were proud of her, too, and delighted in showing her off to our friends. None of them, I fancy, had quite realised what a big boat she was but, of course, we were a big family, and needed a boat of this size. The accommodation amazed everyone, but in the long run it was the boat itself, her obvious strength and stability and seaworthiness, that made the biggest impression. I was often amused to hear some of the less favourably disposed of the fishermen struggling to phrase what they wanted to say – which was on the lines of: 'I don't approve of the Val Bakers, those amateur seamen, but I must admit they've got a good boat there.' That of course, was the unavoidable truth about *Sanu*. She was not only a good boat, she was in fact just the very kind of boat that fishermen liked to see around.

From the beginning the harbour master was very kind to us and did his best to make things as normal as possible, but of course our very size proved something of a handicap. As far as the few large fishing boats were concerned they wished us elsewhere as there always existed the possibility that we occupied space they needed at the quayside – while so far as the small boats were concerned they lived, I think, in secret terror that we would somehow cause them some damage. I could sympathise with both points of view, and yet I could not really agree. A harbour is surely meant for common use, and we should all be able to manage together, working boats and pleasure boats.

Still, apart from a few inevitable pin-pricks we were very happy to be moored at St Ives – and for our children, of course, it was a halcyon period. Day after day they had their friends down and showed them over the boat, or used *Sanu* as a base for bathing when the tide was up. This was the time when our aft cabin came into its own as a sort of club centre. Stephen and his boy friends, Demelza and her girl friends, Genevieve and her younger group of friends – all somehow piled in. And if they weren't there, or bathing, then they would be out rowing in the pram, or persuading Stephen to take them for a run in the motor dinghy.

Meantime Jess and I took advantage of the first opportunity to see *Sanu* in the round, so to speak. At St Ives the harbour dries out, and twice a day *Sanu* was dry, leaning against the quay with a leg out on the other side. We were pleasantly surprised by what we saw when, in some fearfulness, we walked across the sands and stood under the towering hull. Apart from a few barnacles it seemed in excellent condition – and we soon got Stephen and his friends on the job of clearing away the barnacles.

It has been my experience that, as with friends, so with a boat there is no end to the discoveries to be made – and with every experience relationship deepens or collapses. It was so now with *Sanu*. Somehow, being able to see her thus exposed, to stand parallel with the enormous propeller and look at strange bolts and valves and other half hidden attributes normally hidden below the water line – made us much more aware of her as a character. Among other things we got a truer feeling of her size – she really was *vast,* seen out of the water. Indeed she was the biggest of all the St Ives boats to be seen! And she was ours.

'Ah, you've a good boat there,' said Dicky Admiral. 'Take you anywhere – anywhere in the world.'

After that we became more ambitious still in our choices of destination. For one thing, we wanted to achieve something beyond the confinements of coast-hugging: what more natural, then, than a voyage across to the Scillies, the Fortunate Isles? These marvellous little humps, clustering like jewels in the ocean, became a favourite port of call and we had several very pleasant visits, mooring at St Mary's, or over by Trescoe, the island of the marvellous tropical gardens. We had our adventures and alarms, of course, but it was all good experience, and before long we were looking further afield to a long summer voyage up to the Western Isles of Scotland. What a marvellous time we had meandering through the Crinan Canal and then down the Caledonian to Loch Ness itself where Stephen swears he saw the monster. And after that Mull and Skye, Loch Duich and Loch Dunvegan and the castle of Dame Flora MacLeod herself ... It was all real education, for parents and children alike.

And then, after a tentative visit to the Channel Islands, we set out, one Easter, on our most ambitious journey yet – a voyage of more than 1,000 miles, across the English Channel and then up the River Seine to the heart of Paris. There was no doubt that while a few of our ultra-cautious friends looked on us as crazy, most people envied us very much the opportunity – particularly our children's friends who obviously longed to come with us, Alas, we just had not the room, nor could take on the responsibility for such a long trip. As it was, at one time we were committed to taking about 13 people, but in the end two couples dropped out, and the final crew consisted of nine – myself and Jess, Martin and Stephen, Demelza and Genevieve, a young honeymoon couple, Mike and Maureen Richards, and a friend Greta Perry, who volunteered to take on the onerous post of 'galley slave.' This was Jess's idea whose enthusiasm for the trip waned at the thought of having to cook endless meals for nine people: the arrangement of actually employing someone to take on that daily task made an enormous difference, and we were able to really relax from all chores.

As April finally arrived we seemed to be engulfed by the preparations. There were tinned food supplies to be installed, including such items as coffee and tea, which we knew to be either short or very expensive in France. Soon *Sanu's* galley began to look like a shop counter and we wondered if we had overdone things (but in retrospect were rather sorry we had not laid in still more, for prices were to prove exorbitant). Blankets, pillows, sleeping bags, tea cloths, towels, soap ... fuel for the main engine, fuel for the second engine, reserve supplies of oil ... things were run so close that we did not actually test out our new engine until the day before we were due to leave St Ives.

At last, however, it was mid-day on the Saturday, and we all assembled for a last drink at the Sloop, on the waterfront at St

Ives. It was a tantalising sort of day: the sun shone, the sky was blue – but the sea was badly ruffled, and round on the Porthmeor side, definitely disturbed. As we toasted the success of our voyage we were beset with advice from the local fishermen – some saying, 'don't go' – others, knowing our sturdy boat, saying 'Yes, you'll be all right.' In the end after ringing up the coastguards at St Just and making sure there was nothing really dangerous on the way, I decided we should make a start. After all this first leg of the journey from St Ives to Newlyn was the shortest of the whole trip.

Yes, but … ! In fact it proved to be far and away the roughest, as well. From the moment we left St Ives the boat was pitching and rolling and when we got down by Pendeen and rounded Cape Cornwall towards Land's End we were having to take the sea on our beam, which was not at all comfortable. Several of Stephen's school friends had begged to come on this part of the trip round to Newlyn, and I think they began to be rather sorry!

It was just as we were passing the Longships Lighthouse that the unbelievable happened: there was a sudden ominous silence. We looked at one another in consternation. 'The engine's stopped.' Within seconds Mike and I had raced down into the engine room, where we found a scene of minor chaos. The beam seas had been so rough that they had dislodged a 100 gallon water tank, which had in turn knocked a hefty oil drum against the engine – and by an almost incredible bit of bad luck the impact had turned off the tap of the fuel pipe! At such a moment, knowing we were literally only about a hundred yards off the Longships, there was no time to be wasted priming and starting the big engine. Mike and I turned thankfully to our new Lister, he swung with all his might and I pulled over the lever – and, thank goodness, the engine roared into life. Martin at the wheel in the deckhouse was able to steer *Sanu* away from the coast, very slowly of course, while Mike and I turned to the big engine. The trouble was that coming down into the fumes of the engine room was not inducive to a state of peace: before long I had to give way to the inevitable bout of sea-sickness – only the second time I had ever been sick on *Sanu,* and as on the previous occasion, on the first trip of the season. However, after recovering I took turns with Mike at swinging and soon we had the Kelvin roaring into life. Ironically enough, from that moment to the end of the trip three weeks later we never had a moment's worry again from the main engine.

We were certainly glad to get into Newlyn that evening, but soon recovered our spirits with a tot of spirits all round and a big meal. We went to bed early, for we planned to be off at six in the morning – and what's more, so we were. The reason for the early start was that we wanted to go into Salcombe for that evening, as there is a sand bar across Salcombe; with high tide at about three, it was imperative that we reached there not much later than four thirty. Thanks to the extra power of our second engine, which we now had on all the time as well as the main one, we made an excellent run to Salcombe, and though there was quite a swell across the entrance, my familiarity from previous visits made the entry quite straightforward. Not so the problem of anchoring, however. On previous visits we had just dropped our anchor opposite the Marine Hotel and that had been that. On this afternoon there was a very strong wind blowing down the estuary, as well as a heavy swell, and twice we dropped anchor and found it dragging. In the end we managed to get a hold, but just to be on the safe side put out a second anchor.

That evening we had our first real sample of Greta's cooking, and very tasty it was too. We were just sitting back replete afterwards when Martin, who had gone up on deck for a moment, shouted down: 'The dinghy's gone!' We had lowered the big dinghy and left it tied up at the stern – now we found that under the combined strength of wind and swell she had frayed her mooring rope and disappeared into the night. This was a blow indeed, for though we had with us a small Mirror dinghy belonging to Stephen, we relied on the large dinghy for most of our trips ashore. It was dark outside, but we knew that below the ship there were two creeks, and that the dinghy must have floated down and gone ashore somewhere. Mike and Stephen bravely decided to investigate in the small dinghy, and after reluctantly donning life belts, for it was quite nasty out there with the swell, they disappeared into the darkness ... to return an hour later, covered in mud, with no good news to report.

There was nothing left but to sleep on it ... fortunately the next morning there was a chugging noise and the Salcombe harbour-master came alongside us in his launch, accompanied by a familiar figure in the form of Geoff Scott, who had helped us bring *Sanu* down from Southampton a year before. They took Mike and Stephen off in tow for a tour of inspection, and later that morning we witnessed a triumphal return procession – the harbour master's launch towing Mike and Stephen in their dinghy, in turn towing our large white dinghy, looking rather the worse for wear, mud-wise, but intact, even including its engine. This was a great relief, which we celebrated that evening with a drink with Geoff in the King's Arms at Salcombe. Ironically enough, that very afternoon I was sitting on the deck of *Sanu* sunning myself when to my astonishment I saw a small boat floating by – I grabbed a boathook and managed to catch it. Someone else had lost a dinghy in much the same way as ourselves, so we were able to do a good turn to balance our own benefit.

Not only because of losing the dinghy, but owing to a bad weather forecast, we had to spend a day weather-bound in Salcombe. The next forecast was more cheerful, and at seven o'clock in the morning we raised our anchors and crept out of Salcombe and set out across the Channel bound for Cherbourg. We had worked out a course which should bring us on to Cap Hague, and the boat fairly raced along, with a wind behind it ... when at last we spied land we felt rather pleased with ourselves. Then something about the shape began to worry me, and I turned to my invaluable Adlard Cole book, with its photographs of important land marks. Yes, there could be no doubt – that was *not* Cap Hague, it was the Casquets, and we were two or three degrees off course. It was nothing serious; we just altered course slightly and headed on past Alderney and towards Cap Hague, which we could now see ahead. By seven o'clock that evening we had passed on down the French coast and were approaching the big breakwater at Cherbourg, with its convenient landmark of Port D'Est. The entry proved quite simple, what with our course already plotted and Adlard Cole's meticulous series of photographs, and soon we had crossed Petit Rade and found our way to the inner harbour. Here, of course, following extensive correspondence, I fully expected to find someone from the Cherbourg Yacht Club on hand, at least to take a rope. We saw the lines of yachts moored, and edged in, but there was no sign of anyone expecting us, so in the end we made for a long quay beyond, and tied up there for the night. I jumped ashore and ran down to the Yacht Club, a modern and impressive building – to find it all shuttered up and a large sign *Fermez* – apparently closed for a two-day holiday.

Not really downhearted, for we had found a mooring, anyway, we went back to the boat and sat down patiently to await the customs men, for whose benefit we were dutifully flying a yellow flag.

Back home the customs are aboard almost before you have tied up a rope, but here it became obvious, things were different. Nobody was interested. After waiting an hour, we shrugged and gave up, and then we all went ashore to have our first French meal in a Cherbourg restaurant. We were delighted with the swift and efficient service and the tasty dishes, especially the way a succulent soup was brought in a tureen and left for second helpings, but somewhat alarmed by a bill of nearly £10. This was our first experience of a problem that was to haunt us for most of the trip. Prices in France seemed very *very* high: meat, butter, poultry, even cheese and vegetables and fruit – all cost at least twice as much as in England. Bread and milk were more reasonable but there was really only one item which offered a real saving, le Vino. How we enjoyed really being able to indulge ourselves, sampling lovely cool bottles of Alsace or Anjou Rosé or Sylvaner, all at about a quarter of their cost in Britain.

When we returned to *Sanu* for the night we had recovered from the shock of the restaurant bill and all slept very well – to be awoken soon after dawn by bangings on the wheelhouse door. Outside stood several gesticulating fishermen. It appeared we were occupying their traditional berths at the quay and must move at once, so we started up the engine and moved over to a large buoy in the centre of the harbour. Just as we were relaxing again a big launch purred up and a handsome young customs official came aboard looking rather important and demanding to see our documents. At first he was a little grim and stiff, but as soon as his appreciative eye fell upon our pretty young honeymooner, Maureen, relations seemed to improve greatly. In fact the examination was perfunctory; after sampling the prices in France we realised that they were hardly likely to be much worried about anything coming in from their poor cousin Britain.

After a day in Cherbourg we headed off down the French coast for Le Havre, a straight-forward trip provided we managed to find, at the end of it, the Le Havre Light Vessel. It wasn't all that easy, but it helped to know that about every other boat in the vicinity would be heading in much the same direction. From the Light Vessel we altered course for Le Havre itself, quite a tricky approach between two lines of buoys. Once again we had made excellent progress, about 70 miles in eight hours, and after rounding the Digue de Nord we were pleasantly surprised to find a large buoy awaiting just as we had been told by letter. We tied up and looked forward, after a meal, to going ashore by dinghy to explore Le Havre – alas, there was such a big swell coming into the harbour, and we were so exposed to it, that it would have been impossible to go ashore without a great deal of discomfort and inconvenience, so we left it and had an early night, ready for an equally early start in the morning.

At seven we were ready to make our historic entrance into the River Seine, but there were so many large liners queuing up to enter Le Havre that we had to wait our chance for nipping out. Then, when we found the buoys marking the entry to the river, we were a little alarmed to find thick mist forming ahead. I had read that mist was the principal hazard on the Seine and now understood why: it was rather alarming suddenly to find a huge tanker looming out upon us. Fortunately as the morning passed the mist dispersed, and soon we were able to relax. I must say we were all most impressed with the amount of traffic carried on the Seine – we have no river in Britain to compare, from commercial point of view.

Our second favourable impression was the river itself and its lovely background. How pleasant after huge vistas of open sea to see the meandering green hills and wooded valleys, and every now and then a typical riverside town, seeming almost to grow round the water. We stayed our first night at one of these, Duclair, moored up to one of several landing stages. Here we discovered one of the French Co-ops, where prices, particularly of wines, were lower than anywhere else. Despite our linguistic limitations we found no difficulties – there was always pen and paper to work out the prices. In the evening Jess and I and Mike and Maureen escaped for a pleasant drinking session in a riverside cafe where, under the influence of the local vino, we decided gaily that this was the life, this was.

The next morning, starting off in excellent humour, we found after going a mile or two that the new small engine had failed – and that at the same time our bilge pumps had become blocked. We managed to fix the engine but could not at first get the bilges to work – so there was nothing for it but to get the whole ship's company to muster on deck and start operating the four hand-pumps, a truly wearisome task, since each one required about 600 pumps. At the end we walked about with aching muscles. After that Stephen and I vowed we couldn't face it again so we went down into the engine room and took the bilge pumps to pieces, clearing the pipes and then nervously screwing everything back in place. To our joy, they worked at once.

Another set-back awaited us at Rouen, where we had arranged to have our masts lowered. When we pulled into the Dubigen-Normandie boatyard we became alarmed to see large signs of inactivity. When I went to investigate I found that the whole yard was closed down for a four day Easter Holiday. There was nothing for it but a do-it-yourself effort. Michael, who was used to working on fishing boats, worked out a plausible if rather hazardous method of using ropes tied round our anchor winch and gingerly we managed to lower each mast in turn and then get them tied up on our wheel house roof.

Feeling rather pleased with ourselves we set off now through the port of Rouen – which might well have been Southampton, judging by the huge ships lined up, whereas in fact it was 70 miles inland. After a while the big ships were left behind as we began passing under long low bridges, and soon we were out of Rouen and heading up river. All at once the nautical environment changed: there were no more huge liners, but in their place literally dozens and dozens of long low steel barges, used for carrying cargoes not only up to Paris but on and through waterways all over France. Each seemed to be operated by a couple and their family – many of them had long lines of washing drying on the decks, and children running around. Most of these barges were twice as long as our own boat and when, as often was the case, they were lashed together in fours or sixes, pushed by a tug, they made a formidable sight. When loaded they would sink so low in the water that it was quite easy to miss seeing them altogether. Altogether I found navigation on the Seine was far trickier than I had imagined, and was very glad of my detailed charts. On the other hand the French waterways arrangements seem very thorough; the most detailed systems were worked out, so that boats going one way went under one arch of a bridge, and boats coming down under another. We never had any real trouble, and found the barge skippers a friendly lot, usually exchanging waves as we passed. Perhaps because it was early in the season we were actually the only pleasure boat seen on the river either going to Paris or returning.

That night we reached our first lock, at Amfreville de Poses, and tied up by a barge. The next day, Easter Sunday, we set off early hoping perhaps to reach Paris. We were now passing through beautiful stretches of countryside, with great châteaux perched on the tops of hills and vast stretches of sheer green fields. We travelled about 25 miles to the next lock – and then found it was closed for the day. There was nothing for it but to pull in and tie up to a single barge that was moored by the river bank. We came alongside carefully and Stephen jumped aboard the barge to tie a rope ... A few moments later I found two sad looking figures gesticulating from the barge wheelhouse, the woman pointing ... at the remains of a milk pudding she had put out to cool, and upon which Stephen had firmly stepped. We hastily sent over a tin of fruit as a peace offering, and in fact, despite the unfortunate introduction, we soon made friends. They were charming people, a couple who talked to us about their life taking loads up and down the

French waterways: mostly their cargo seemed to consist of oats and barley, for export to British whisky makers!

At one stage the skipper took us down into his engine room. It was spotlessly clean, putting ours to shame – there was even a big panel with a slot for every single tool in the right place, which I eyed with envy thinking of our regrettable habit of removing tools and forgetting to return them. Unlike our cumbersome hand-starting of the Kelvin, the barge skipper had an air-starting system; just a flick and a twirl, and she was purring away. The domestic quarters were quite large, too, and obviously their life was quite a comfortable one.

To pass the time we all went for a long walk in the picturesque Normandy countryside. It appeared a well-to-do area, and we kept coming upon one huge villa after another, many of them obviously used as week-end retreats. Everywhere there were tables and chairs in the gardens and people relaxing in the sudden sunshine. We walked on, and Maureen picked a large bunch of wild May blossom. As we returned the barge skipper's wife smiled and said rather sweetly, 'Ah we call those the flowers of love.'

Easter Monday was the day we had planned to reach Paris, and we made a very great effort, starting at seven in the morning and covering 100 miles by dusk. This entailed passing through several of the huge French locks, most of which have three chambers, and house half a dozen enormous barges at a time. I must admit I felt nervous for *Sanu's* safety, crammed between the slimy lock walls and a huge steel barge, but we survived. On and on we pounded, not only with both main and second engine going, but also with our generator humming away, for we found on such a voyage, with long evenings in the saloon, we used up electricity at an alarming rate. When we passed through the lock at Bougail, some 45 kilometres from Paris, at about six we thought perhaps we might reach our destination, but in the end we reached the last lock at Suresnes just too late, to find everything shut up. We had to pass an impatient night there, one that was greatly relieved by a truly magnificent spaghetti dish made by our ever-improving chef. At first, I think she felt overwhelmed, but later became very efficient at whipping up meals for nine and even at one period eleven.

All the way up the Seine the weather had not been too kind, and now, as if determined to serve up a spectacular finale, it worsened. When, early the next morning, we took our place in the Suresenes lock for the last passage it was already raining heavily. Afterwards, as we began passing Bois de Boulogne and there ahead of us saw the famed shape of the Eiffel Tower – now, of all times, the rain turned to sleet, and as at last we approached the Pont Alexandre and headed for the Touring Club de France, it was actually *snowing*.

Fortunately when nine people have survived crossing the English Channel and several more days at sea and journeying up river in a comparatively small boat, their spirits are not going to be dampened by rain or snow. There was a slight pause as somewhat astonished officials of the Touring Club of France held a debate about what to do with our rather bulky *Sanu,* then they finally found us a perfect site at the quayside. By mid-day on our first morning we had all taken advantage of the excellent shower facilities provided, and emerged sartorially splendrous, ready to see the sights.

Our position at the Port de Plaisance, close to the Quai D'Orsay, was pretty convenient all round: a short stroll brought us to Champs Elysées and bus and metro soon took us further afield. There were often times when Jess and I wished that we were on our own, to be really free to wander at will and enjoy the numerous wonders of Paris. On the other hand, we were pleased to find that the children really did enjoy the novelty of the experience. In particular we were interested at their reaction when taken into the big art galleries like the Louvre – they were constantly tugging at our sleeves and demanding that we came to see the Mona Lisa or some other famous picture, which to them had previously been just a name in a book. I think we were all most thrilled by a visit to the main Impressionist Exhibition, in a wing of the Louvre. It was a truly sensual pleasure to walk up a staircase and see a grand vista of Van Goghs or the wondrous hazy landscapes of Monet or the lovely Renoir and Degas nudes – all in their original canvases.

Day after day during our stay in Paris the wind blew, the rain rained and once more the snow snowed – but there were patches of sunshine, and not even bad weather could obliterate the visual delights. For us, two experiences helped to confirm this. First, the traditional visit to the Eiffel Tower: we found the queuing intolerable, indeed everything about the organised interminable trip upwards quite exasperating – but once at the top we forgave all for the wonderful view. From there one comprehended the magical and truly beautiful layout of Paris. We could only take our photographs and marvel, and come down again. Our other, more intimate view, was during a leisurely ride in one of the old horse-drawn carriages that park by the Champs Elysées. It was a delightful ride, past the Arc de Triomphe and then through the leafy Bois de Boulogne.

Another memorable occasion was when I piloted our large party out to a Montparnasse cinema to see a performance of Jacques Tati in *Jour de Fête*. We were unprepared for the gaiety with which the cinema staff had planned the evening. Not only was the cinema foyer specially decorated, but before the main film there was a sudden burst of music and in marched a brass band, obviously based on the one in the film, to entertain us for half an hour ... and when they left dozens of bright balloons were hurled down on the audience from the gallery by the attendants. Our English film shows are never such fun!

Our children had several outings of their own, including a visit to the Olympia to hear Les Kinks. Over in Britain, of course, such groups were very popular, with the result that many of our teenage boys had long hair, our son Stephen being no exception. In France, obviously, this was still a rarity, and in one restaurant the manager, with a mischevious smile approached Stephen brandishing a large pair of scissors.

Most of our shopping for the boat, while in Paris, was done in Rue St Dominique, just across the river, where we found prices more reasonable. We would have liked to eat out more but funds simply would not permit; however, we did enjoy two special evenings. The first was for the whole company, nine of us along with two friends who were visiting us – we decided on this occasion to follow the advice of one of the tourist leaflets and visit one of those restaurants which offer a special tourist meal at a price of about 8 francs a head. By the time we had ordered half a dozen bottles of wine, of course, the cost had risen considerably, but we did feel we had value for money. This was the evening when, like proper tourists, we roamed about the brightly lit streets of Montmartre, and a goggle-eyed Stephen was enticed into one of the strip clubs by an apparent charge of only 2 francs 50 cents – soon to emerge very indignant at being asked 20 francs for a glass of orangeade! It was also the evening, regrettably, when our 13 year old teenager, Demelza, partook of more *rosé* than was good for her, and on the way home, much to our embarrassment, kept declaring at the top of her young voice: '*Down* with de Gaulle!'

Our other evening was a more private one, just Jess and I and Mike and Maureen. We strolled past Notre Dame and found a delightful red-table-cloth restaurant by the edge of the river, where we wined and dined excellently, ending up dancing with the manager and other diners, to the strains of an Italian accordionist. Afterwards a taxi back to Port de Plaisance and then we all leaned over the bridge looking down on the waters of the Seine, now sparkling with reflected lights – and there, below us, the warm friendly glow of our own sturdy boat, *Sanu*. These are the moments one remembers dearly after voyaging abroad in your own boat.

Our trip back down the Seine was much quicker than the upward one, for of course we now had the current with us. Indeed we travelled much of the way at the startling speed of 12 knots an hour, passing most of the heavily laden barges. The sun was shining at long last and we were relaxing thinking to ourselves, we know the route, nothing much can go wrong … At last as dusk approached we decided to pull in behind a row of barges waiting for the morning for the lock ahead. On this occasion Mike was at the wheel, so I went forward with a rope, ready to jump ashore. As *Sanu* glided in closer and closer to the bank I stood idly waiting, watching the rear of the steel barge coming nearer, and waiting, for Mike to put the boat into reverse. I waited … and waited … and suddenly, with a terrifying movement, *Sanu* seemed to leap forward and went straight into the back of the barge! The moment is etched into my mind: I could not really believe my eyes. What had happened of course has happened to me – in a momentary confusion Mike put the gear into forward instead of reverse, and by the time he corrected the mistake it was too late.

The next few moments were rather comic. Apparently the crew of the barge must have been asleep, for there was silence for a few horrified moments, and then they came rushing on deck, gesticulating and making anguished movements of their hands. Mike and I stood there apologising profusely, and it did not help to discover they knew not a word of English. At last when they had calmed down the skipper demanded that we accompany him to make an official report. By now it was dark, and rather miserably Mike and I followed him along the tow path and across the lock chambers to the offices of the head lock-keeper. Here a real pantomime took place, with the lock-keeper and the skipper knowing no English, and Mike and me pretty ill-equipped with French ... between us we had to fill up about four official forms, including lengthy descriptions of our boat and what had happened. By the time it was all over Mike and I crawled back exhausted. Even then we had had to promise that one of us would be available at six in the morning for an official measurement of the damaged parts of the barge. Mike took on this task, and later when we came down for breakfast we found him rather dazed – apparently the occasion had been more token than important; afterwards they had all sat down and drank whisky together!

We were glad to press on the next day, and went as far down the river as Villequiex, not far from the estuary mouth. Here we had an early night hoping to make a good start in the morning ... but awoke to find the boat completely shrouded in mist, with traffic on the river at a standstill. It was very eerie and impossible, and we were just resigning ourselves to spending the day there, when, about ten o'clock, the mist quite abruptly cleared. I was uneasy about making Cherbourg before dark with such a late start, but we decided to try. We then set off on what was probably the most wonderful day of the whole trip, gliding in brilliant sunshine to the mouth of the Seine and then on over a dead calm sea to Cape Barfleur. Just in case we got caught out in the dark I had swotted up the lights of the relevant buoys, and now I was glad I had, for dusk quickly turned into dark ...

However, rounding the Cape I was able to identify the first buoy, and then the second, and headed for the third, beyond which Cherbourg lay only two miles away – and then, somehow, I couldn't find it. Suddenly, what had been all peaceful and pleasant, for me at any rate, turned into a minor nightmare. My eyesight is not so good now, and we have a rather weak light on our compass anyway, so that all at once I was having to put on glasses to read the compass then take them off again to look ahead at the bewildering vista of lights that indicated Cherbourg. Jess was with me for a time but I was becoming irritable now, and after a few exchanges she retired in high dungeon leaving me to bring *Sanu* into harbour in the dark on my own – a state of responsibility which worried me still more. Martin came up to keep me company and between us we tried to identify a wandering winking red light and a green light in the right position, which would indicate the eastern approach to Cherbourg. However, the nearer we got the less I liked the look of the surrounding vague shadowy shapes, that could well be that cursed breakwater ... Finally I swung the boat away, thinking better to be safe than sorry.

At this stage Mike came up and kindly took over the wheel while I retired to make an intensive study of our charts for every scrap of information about the night entry into Cherbourg. In the end wisely as it happened, we decided to take a bit longer and make for the western entrance, which was more easily indentifiable by a winking light. At long last, with Mike confidently handling the wheel and more than atoning for his momentary lapse of a day ago, we crept into Cherbourg – two hours later than we should have been, but at least intact.

Our last morning was devoted to raising our masts again, then we pooled all our remaining francs and centimes and bought a last few bottles of wine. At two thirty in the afternoon we set off homeward bound with both engines roaring away, steaming on and on down the English Channel right through the night – our second trip since acquiring the boat. They were not such pleasant conditions as the return from the Channel Islands, indeed it was Force 5-6 most of the way, but we made much quicker progress thanks to the other engine. Also this time we had the sense to organise a system of watches, so that two of us were on for three hours, and then off for six. Finally at about eight in the morning we sighted high land which we hoped was the Lizard, but proved to be cliffs more towards Falmouth. But at least we were not far off; five hours later we had rounded Land's End and were actually heading into St Ives Bay – where we had to anchor for a couple of hours before being able to make our final landfall in the harbour.

By that time the various coast guards must have passed their message round, for though I have never before seen a customs man at St Ives, there was one waiting to jump aboard to check on us and our cargo. So ended a trip which none of us would have missed for the world, despite bad weather – and from which, parents and children alike, I think learned a good deal about our neighbour, France, than would be possible from any more conventional form of travel.

Part Four

Up Our Very Own Creek

I

Paradise Creek

I suppose on the face of it there was no reason why St Christopher's should not have remained our family home forever ... but the simple fact is, quite suddenly, I found myself becoming aware of a strange kind of restlessness, which I had not felt for many, many years. I recognised that in fact I had been experiencing twinges of this same sensation for some time past: but now, all at once, it came sweeping over me like long regular waves ... and at last one day I said to Jess, not quite sure I was hearing myself right, 'What do you say – shall we sell the house?'

In fact it wasn't such an abrupt idea as perhaps it sounded. During the past few years at St Christopher's, although it might be said we had acquired a seventh child in the form of *Sanu,* it could also not be denied that one by one our children had been making their departures. Now there was only Stephen, already half way through an A level course which should shortly take him to university, and Genevieve. This would mean eventually only three of us, with the somehow daunting prospect of life in a huge 16-roomed house. Well, if the imagination was not stirred by such a prospect, then a thoughtful walk around the house would certainly do the trick. Bedroom after bedroom empty and somehow rather sterile, inhabited perhaps by the ghostly spirits of Martin, of Gill, of Jane, of Demelza, yet almost painfully and visibly devoid of their real and lively personalities. And then there was that 30-foot sitting room, scene of so many family gatherings and parties, how vast and solitary it often seemed!

'Yes,' said Jess thoughtfully. 'You could be right at that.'

Thus simply, in effect, did we signal the beginning of the end of a decade of life together, for it was nearly ten years since we had first settled in St Ives. I have often found this to be the way our family life has progressed, changing course every now and then almost casually, it might seem – though in fact the end decision is really the product of some deep-seated subterranean thinking. In this case I am sure that the possibility of an eventual move must have been hovering in the back of our minds for some time, and not only because of the prospect of a dwindling family.

Of course, a decision made is one thing – putting it into practice quite another, as we were now to find out. In all it took us more than a year and all kinds of complicated arrangements before we finally managed to find a purchaser for our old home.

In the meantime, we had begun the task of finding a new one. In some ways, I suppose, it was a similar situation to the time when we decided to buy our own boat. We knew we wanted a boat, had a fairly good idea of the kind of boat we would like, but found the only way to go about matters was to start looking around, following up advertisements, agents reports and so forth.

So now the obvious first step was to approach local estate agents, and of course study those ever fascinating classified columns of the local newspapers. But even before doing that it was essential to have a clear idea of what we were looking for.

'Well, you should know,' said Jess with a disdainful sniff. 'It's all your idea to uproot yourself like this. Just when I was looking forward to peaceful retirement, too.'

Fortunately I did not need to pay much attention to such remarks. I recognised them as forming part of the mutual duelling that Jess and I engage in over any major change in our lives, each taking an opposite stance, often reversing it, generally enjoying the bantering exchange. Underneath it all, one knew, the way lay forward.

'Well, let's think about our future plans,' I said. 'Just what are they?'

'I know what mine are – I'm fed up with living by the sea, I want to see lots of green things and grow my own food … in short I want to live in the country.'

'I agree entirely,' I said. 'But I think it stands to reason that, in looking for our new home, we should take into account something besides our own immediate needs.'

'What do you mean?' said Jess, as if she didn't know.

I meant, of course, *Sanu*. Ever since we had acquired her some three years previously our great dream had been some kind of way of keeping the boat as handily as one keeps a car. Alas, our situation at St Ives, with its uncomfortable ground-swell harbour, had not been an encouraging one. On the few occasions we had brought the boat into the harbour she had received quite a bit of buffeting alongside the quay, and she was too big for a mooring in that small space. Consequently we had been driven to seek a series of temporary homes – at Hayle, at Newlyn, at Falmouth, finally in a snug haven at Flushing. But the last was about 22 miles away, which created a lot of difficulties.

How different all this would be if we were able to keep *Sanu* literally at the bottom of the garden. It did not look possible to do this at St Ives, or indeed anywhere in the Penwith area. We had, indeed, tried to get a permanent berth at Newlyn and Penzance inner harbours, but were refused these by the harbour-masters who felt that space should only be given to commercial vessels. But it might well be possible to find somewhere suitable up the River Fal or one of its tributaries, somewhere like that.

And so, suddenly presented with a unifying theme for our house searching, we seemed to spring into action. At least things were certainly much clearer. We had made up our minds to leave St Christopher's – and we wanted our new home to be a countrified place literally at the water's edge.

One day, browsing through a current issue of *Yachting World,* I came upon an unusual advertisement of a waterside property for sale in South Cornwall – in fact, a complete creek, including, and this is what made my eyebrows rise excitedly, its own quays.

'South Cornwall,' I said slowly, showing the advertisement to Jess. 'Of course that could be pretty well anywhere. There's only a box number. Still, you never know. I'll write off and see.'

A few days later there arrived in the post two very detailed foolscap typewritten sheets giving us the very fullest gen on 'The Old Sawmills, Golant, Near Fowey.' The opening paragraphs, or what I suppose in advertising parlance might be called the introductory blurb, ran as follows:

Situated on the south side of a small creek off the River Fowey, about one mile up river from Port, Yachting Centre and Holiday resort of Fowey, and half a mile down river from the pretty little village of Golant.

Access to the property is by a footpath from Fowey to Golant which passes across the head of the creek. But the shortest route to the nearest road is to follow the West Bank of the river alongside the railway line to Golant. This takes an average of ten minutes. Negotiations with the landowner of the adjoining land to allow a driveway to be made across his land from the road to the property are being made. A diesel crawler tractor, complete with hydraulics and bulldozer blade, was purchased so that the majority of the levelling work could be carried out by the owner.

It cannot be over-stressed that this is one of the quietest and prettiest spots in the country, with the creek in front of the house, the tide is in for about six hours, and out for about six hours, the steep slope of Golant Downs across the creek rising to the sky, and the thickly wooded slopes of Colvithick Woods behind the house.

The house built of stone, about 1600, is partly living accommodation, partly workshop. The living accommodation could be extended into the workshop if desired.

Then followed a description of the accommodation of the house, leading to a note about a large workshop with a loft floor, containing a $4\frac{1}{2}$ h.p. diesel engine driving a generator and circular saw.

But it was the second sheet that really intrigued us, for on this were listed details of a fantastic series of miscellaneous external buildings, etc. These included three complete chalets, all quite large, two of them with two bedrooms each, and fully equipped with furniture and electricity; a 4-berth house boat,

completely equipped, with calor gas cooking; a 12-foot
4-seater fibreglass boat with outboard; a 13-foot clinker
inboard motor a 16-foot fireglass sheathed hull and large
outboard; the Bristol Diesel crawler tractor, complete with
hydraulics and bulldozer blades; a large motor mower; a fire
pump complete with fire hoses, and a huge list of tools of
various sorts. Finally, the quays were mentioned (all grassed)
and the fact that there was a large orchard among the $2\frac{1}{2}$ acres
of land.

I must admit that, with my essentially romantic nature, the
whole thing sounded rather fascinating – though of course, I
told myself, Fowey was far too distant a place, and really out of
the question. All the same at least it would make an unusual
Sunday outing. So I rang up Mr Bishop, the owner, and made
an appointment to view the following Sunday. Just before
ringing off I checked on that bit about the approach – yes,
there really wasn't any other way, but it was quite easy to
follow the railway line … This is just what we found ourselves
doing the following Sunday. It was a lovely sunny day in
October, and once we had driven down the tortuous winding
lane into Golant and seen the wide estuary spread out ahead of
us we had been put into a good mood. Now, leaving our car by
the disused railway halt, we began walking alongside the railway
track that ran literally along the water's edge towards Fowey.

'It's certainly a beautiful setting,' said Jess. 'Look at the way
those fields rise up on the other side, and all those trees.'

It was indeed very beautiful. The river itself, too, was most
attractive as it wound down towards Fowey – at the bottom,
where it turned we could see quite a few large boats at
moorings, and also the funnels of one of the big china clay
cargo boats.

We began walking along the railway line. From where we
stood it appeared to follow a curve right round to Fowey, and
there was no evidence of any building.

'Are you sure you've got the right directions?' said Jess.
'Never mind – it's a lovely day for an outing. Here, let's pick
some blackberries.'

I can remember becoming quite irritated by the
blackberry-picking. We had come to view property I reminded

Jess and Stephen, *not* to gallivant about; and I marched on purposefully, the others trailing a little behind me.

And then – well, then, all at once, the land to the right of me fell away unexpectedly – the railway line abruptly revealed itself as running on across two small bridges – and there, to our right, opening out in all its sunlit glory, was the creek – or Bodmin Pill, as we discovered it was to be called.

Of course, it was high tide, which showed everything off at its best, but neither Jess nor I would ever forget that first view; the long stretch of calm water leading up to the tiny quays, rising up above them first one of the chalets, and then – nestling as if growing naturally out of the surrounding countryside, the pink-washed granite shape of the Old Sawmills, a thin column of smoke curling up from its main chimney.

'Why,' said Jess, suddenly lost for words. 'Why … '

For a brief moment we exchanged excited looks, then we turned and began hurrying on to where a gate opened into the woods and there was obviously a footpath leading along the creek. Neither of us said anything then, but we were both aware, perhaps somewhat apprehensively, that something strange and perhaps eventful was happening.

Taking the winding footpath we came at last to a small sign, 'The Old Sawmills,' and went through a wicker gate and along a path that sloped downwards towards the pink cottage. Even so as we drew level we were still above the house, and could look down upon a rather idyllic scene: a baby asleep in a pram in the sunny garden, half shaded by a large beach tree, on the quay below a bonfire burning up the weeds, the outline of three small boats lying at the quays.

Mr and Mrs Bishop were waiting to show us round. They were much younger than we had expected, and indeed had a very young family of four girls from seven down to a few months old. These latter, we gathered, were the real reason for their decision to sell up; with such small children life in such an isolated spot was inevitably complicated. But during the years they had lived there, Mr Bishop now hastened to assure us, they had carried out quite a lot of improvements and had built up quite a useful trade in holiday lettings of the chalets.

He showed us a guide-book illustrated with a beguiling view of
the creek and containing several scraps of local information
which I found interesting – such as the fact that as far back as
1400 the merchants of Bodmin used to use the creek for the
shipment of their goods, but 'the activity of those days had
now yielded to a tranquillity and softness matched only by the
surrounding beauty' and, listing the many lovely creeks up the
River Fowey, the booklet painted a vivid picture of 'Lerryn
Creek with its great woods and trees overhanging the still, dark
water; Pont Pill, sombre and quiet; and Penal Creek, severe
and imposing ... while Golant with its little church where King
Mark and Queen Iseult came to worship invites closer
acquaintance.'

While, of course, this was, strictly speaking, sales talk, I
could not help responding, feeling it really was on the right
lines. It would be no good viewing the Old Sawmills by any
normal standards, it was not a normal sort of place. Some
weeks later, by a coincidence, a middle-aged couple came to
view St Christopher's and it transpired that quite recently they
had also viewed the Old Sawmills. They were obviously
horrified at the prospect of living in such a remote place ...
whereas in fact, to me, it was the very remoteness that was its
attraction.

And not only to me, I was pleased to discover. When, a
couple of hours later, we were once again walking away down
the railway track – after thoroughly exploring the three chalets,
the boats, the workshop, the orchard and even the fresh-water
stream which provided the water, piped down to the house –
we stopped to take a last look back.

'Well?' I said, looking at Jess uncertainly.

There was no answer for a while, and I went on
uncomfortably.

'Anyway, you must admit, it's interesting to *see* these places.
After all – '

I stopped then because Jess was speaking at last. Her eyes
were bright and she looked quite bemused.

'Oh, but I think it's *marvellous,*' she said. 'I just couldn't
believe my eyes.'

'What – you mean?'

'How much are you going to offer?' said Jess eagerly.

And on that note we walked on down the railway track, back to our car and the 50-mile journey to St Ives.

*

The next day I made my offer to Mr Bishop. Taking everything into consideration I felt it was quite a fair one, but as I feared he adopted the inevitable counter-position and said it wasn't enough, and the next two or three weeks were spent in the usual fencing that goes on with any property sale. I couldn't help being amused at our differing techniques. My method, inevitably I suppose for an author, was to compose a long and eloquent letter setting out all the reasons why I really could not see my way to offer more than so much. I put quite a lot of time and thought into those letters. Mr Bishop, on the other hand, seldom wrote letters: he merely picked up the telephone and rang me and said he was sorry he couldn't accept my offer. I then wrote another eloquent letter offering a little more. Finally, and rather surprisingly, Mr Bishop indicated the lowest figure he was willing to take, which was still quite a lot more than I felt like paying. More eloquent letters, and then a rather ominous silence from Mr Bishop. Finally somewhat grudgingly I offered the figure Mr Bishop had stipulated as his lowest. The next morning the phone rang.

'It's a deal,' said Mr Bishop. 'I'll get my solicitors to start drawing up the contract at once.'

*

The moment we were thus committed, of course, I began to have not merely, second, but third, fourth, and fifth thoughts. What on earth was I proposing to do – uprooting ourselves from a nice sociable place like St Ives, with every convenience to hand, and dumping us down in this remote and very inconvenient spot?

What about all our friends living mainly in and around St Ives – or certainly within the loose confines of what is termed West Penwith? Removing ourselves to Fowey on the South Coast meant putting a solid 50 miles between ourselves and the area that had been home territory for practically the whole 18 years of our married life. We must be mad!

And then there were the sheer physical problems involved. The Old Sawmills was completely inaccessible by car, the only approach was either a 10 minute walk along the railway line or via a muddy footpath, or by boat from Golant down river and up the creek – and this last method was only viable when the tide was in. What about delivering heavy objects, or even bringing home the shopping – wasn't it going to be somewhat complicated, not to say arduous? And then, when one actually got to the house there remained other problems – water for instance. No mains water out here in the wooded wilds – the water supply was a freshwater stream that ran down through Gollethick Wood, and the method of distraction was disarmingly simple – a plastic pipe was bedded into the stream 1,000 feet up the valley and this fed water down into two water tanks which in turn fed water into the three chalets and the main house. It was all done by gravity and seemed almost too simple; uneasily I felt that, with someone like me in charge, hidden snags might be found.

Fortunately mains electricity was already laid on, while in case it should fail there was always calor gas, and in general the house and chalets were quite well equipped. Nevertheless it was not difficult to keep thinking up possible snags ... and then, finally, there were the especially complicated problems provided, for the moment, by our remaining two-home-based children, Stephen and Genevieve. Stephen had recently passed eight 'O' levels and was now embarked on a two-year course at the Humphry Davy Grammar School, Penzance: he was very happily settled there, it would be obviously foolish to move him at this stage. The best arrangement for him would be to board somewhere during the week and come to us at Fowey for the long week-ends. Fortunately we knew he could stay at the home of one of his best friends, and so there were no real worries.

But Genevieve presented quite a problem. Although twelve she was already very much a teenager, and her social life in St Ives appeared a thriving one – she did not like the idea of disturbing it one iota. On the other hand we had to hesitate before the idea of taking her to live at the Old Sawmills and going to the local school at Fowey, for it would involve a most complicated journey by foot along the railway line, and self-evidently she would be rather lonely. Besides, she, too, was very happy at her school at Penzance, St Clare's. Here again the sensible compromise solution came up, that Genny should become a weekly boarder at St Clare's, coming home every week-end with Stephen.

One way and another, what with these problems and several others provided by our attempts to find a new home for the pottery and a purchaser for St Christopher's, the whole business of moving often got us right down. I know that for weeks I found it difficult to sleep at night; I would toss and turn contemplating the endlessly involved situations that would arise if we moved to Fowey. It did not make matters any simpler that, with the pottery moving to Penzance, Jess would still have to continue there for another year at least before her planned selling-out of her share. This meant she would have to spend three days a week in Penzance, away from Fowey, and I would be left there in solitary state – Oh, no, it just was too complicated.

Many times I am sure we were almost on the point of giving up in the face of so many problems, but always one very simple thing stopped us. Every week or so I arranged with Mr Bishop to go over to Fowey to spend a few hours becoming familiar with the general layout of things ... and by a quirk of fate on each of those occasions the sun rode high in the blue sky, the tide was usually up, and the moment we set foot on that railway track and walked down that beautiful riverside walk – above all when we came suddenly in sight of the Old Sawmills, nestling against the quiet background of dark green trees – well, there could be no doubt about it, both Jess and I felt all our doubts melting away. Come what may, we would be fools not to grasp such an opportunity. Away with doubtings and half heartedness! Be daring! Take the leap into the unknown!

And so, inexorably, the movement accelerated from vague possibility to near-achievement. Our solicitors began the usual inquiries and searches, as a result of which one day there arrived in the post some fascinating photostat copies of plans and deeds and other information ... One factor about which we had been particularly concerned was the outer quay of the property which, unlike the others, was actually set on the main river side of the railway, and had obviously been used by the sawmills in the old days for loading on to large coasting ships for transport further afield. It was this quay that had caught my eyes in the first place, for if it were possible to tie *Sanu* up there then she really would be at the bottom of the garden. Unfortunately the quay was in what might be called a state of some disrepair, many of the top slabs having fallen into the river, and it would need quite a lot of work doing to it first, while the sandy bed would need clearing, too. Nevertheless, there were hopeful possibilities – and now, thank goodness, the documents showed that there were no ownership problems.

One day our solicitor decided to take a look round the property, and this I found illuminating, for of course his expert eye was able to notice many small points that might have escaped our attention. It became obvious that by his more sophisticated and purely legal standards we were paying a rather high price for such an inaccessible property: on the other hand he agreed with my point that what really counted was what a place was worth to the particular person purchasing. I did in fact think that we were paying rather more than we should have done; on the other hand there really had seemed no alternative, and anyway now the deed was done.

Not quite, of course, for house purchasing is never a simple affair, and this one least of all. There was a problem over responsibility for electricity supply, and then the Bishops were held up in their own property arrangements, so that one way and another several months went by before we could finalise everything. In the meantime, in view of the difficulties of transporting heavy articles to the Old Sawmills, I was trying to work out long lists of everything we would need beforehand, so that one move could cover the lot. In particular Jess was very keen that we should replace the existing small kitchen with a larger one, and this could be done fairly simply by building a floor over the workshop. We had studied this problem and it seemed straightforward enough, but it involved us taking with us eleven 20-foot beams plus 160 15-foot lengths of tongue and grooving, not to mention sacks of cement and sand and so on ... There was also the question of heating the chalets, which our children were determined to have for themselves, so we had ordered three Courtier stoves and pipings – all this would have to be gathered together, too.

Then there was the question of the actual move itself. It wasn't going to be like any other move we had made. Even when we had lived in Peter's Cottage on the cliffs at Sennen Cove, the furniture van had been able to back right up to the short path leading into the cottage. But at Golant the furniture van was going to be able to reach the railway halt, and no further. At that point it would be necessary to move all the furniture from the van and put it into a boat, for travelling down river, under the bridge and up to the quay nearest to the house. Quite a prospect!

Fortunately all these matters could be resolved. We booked a large furniture van from Penzance, and then, via the Bishops, were put on to John Fuge at Golant, a local boat builder who had a large flat bottom boat and would be happy to oblige.

For a long time the moving date seemed ages away. Then suddenly it loomed nearer, much nearer. Three weeks, two weeks, one week – all became pandemonium. In the middle of all this we were trying to have friends round for farewell meals and get-togethers; there were strangers constantly coming to look over our own house, which had still not been sold; and we had the problem of deciding whether to try and let it furnished for the summer months or not.

When the day finally came for our move we felt a reasonable sense of confidence if only because we and the furniture removers had taken the precaution of loading up the previous day. It had been quite a business, too, but by late afternoon the van was packed tight. Just before they drove off to Penzance for the night the removers were given strict instructions as to how to get to Golant early the next morning.

'And don't forget, you *must* reach Golant by mid-day, so that we can take advantage of the high tide for doing the boat trips.'

No, they promised, they wouldn't forget. And they didn't either. I know they made a nice early start – if only because, passing through Hayle about eleven o'clock the next morning, I caught a horrified glimpse of the big, familiar lorry parked in a garage forecourt, with jacks underneath and a wheel off ... In fact, to tell the truth the sight, and its implications, was so upsetting that I pretended to myself it had been a hallucination and drove on, with Jess and Genevieve and Stephen and his friend, Nicky, bound for Golant. When we reached there about mid-day we found John Fuge and his helpers awaiting us, looking just a little anxious.

'Hope the furniture men won't be long. The tide, you see.'

Alas the furniture men were long – one hour, two hours, nearly three hours after the time fixed. However, at last the van chugged down into Golant and reversed up to the railway. An alarming sight it made, too, for large quantities of beams and planking, as well as a small electric pottery kiln, had been packed to one side, so that the van heeled over drunkenly, like a ship going before the wind at sea.

'Back axle'll go in a moment,' observed someone caustically, but at least we were spared that. It transpired that the removers, starting off early as promised, had had not one but *two* punctures, necessitating the sending out for a replacement wheel from the Penzance depot before they could get going.

Anyway, there was no time for recriminations: time – and, especially, the tide – waited for no man. Quickly we began unloading what was in the van, carrying it across the railway tracks, and down the quay at Golant to where John Fuge's not over-large red boat waited to take on this rather unusual load.

I could see that John and his helpers were a little taken aback at the variety of our load – two pianos, ten sacks of cement, a harp, a potter's kiln, 88 lengths of timber, just to mention a few – but they set to and soon had the first boatload aboard. In the meantime Stephen and Nicky, got our 'Zodiac' blown up and roared away down river to open up the house, while Jess and Genny plodded along the railway track on the first of several trips.

By now it was nearly high tide, so that the number of journeys that could be made would be seriously curtailed. Fortunately the boat, though small, held quite a good load, and during the afternoon we were able to make three full trips

– though the last two were somewhat nervous ones as the tide was falling, and on the last occasion we had quite a job to lift sacks of cement out of the boat onto our quay, now several feet higher than the boat. Here John Fuge, a man of massive strength, was a great encouragement, apparently thinking nothing of picking up bags of cement as if they were filled with feathers. Even he, though, was fooled by one of several tea-chests I had filled with books – going to pick it up airily and then being stuck, with a comic look of dismay on his face.

Actually the move had not been as complicated as it might have been, as for the moment we had left some of our furniture at St Christopher's including, notably, our huge Welsh dresser. The prospect of sailing down the river with a Welsh dresser broadside would have daunted anyone, I think. I was reminded of a story told by one of the local men of when he helped to move the belongings of another author, the late Leo Walmsley, who also lived up a creek, off Polruan – and how they balanced a piano on a floating pontoon, floating sedately across the river mouth. It must have made an amusing sight – and so did one of our pianos, which we had left on the quay, when the high tide lapped around the bottom, and Stephen donned wellingtons and sat playing!

Fortunately the piano was the only item we failed to get up the winding steps to the house – but, oh, what a tiring task! Unused as we were to physical labour, we ached and creaked all over for days after. Indeed by the end I was reduced to emptying my tea chests of their contents in feeble armfuls.

But at least, by the evening, miraculously, we were in. Almost the first thing we had carried up had been the bright new orange carpet we had bought from the sitting room, together with our round table and suite from St Christopher's … Jess and Genevieve managed to carry these up, and in no time we had a homely sitting-room, with a fire burning and an air, already, of being lived in. We were glad of the fire, as it was still March, but constantly we found our gazes straying to the windows – for with the tide still partially in, and the trees sprouting their early green, the creek made a lovely sight, especially to eyes starved of foilage from the wind-swept northern coast.

Later that evening, after a meal, we strolled down to the quay – *our* quay. By now it was dark, but, appropriately, a spring moon had appeared, its silvery light falling over everything like a magic wand. Genevieve had gone to bed, exhausted, and Stephen was pottering about in the workshop that was to be his especial delight, so for a moment Jess and I were alone. We stood by the quay's side, looking down to where the main River Fowey flowed past the railway bridge.

'Well,' said Jess, 'we're here. Did you ever believe we would be?'

Curiously enough, I had always been pretty certain, if only because I knew in my heart that the time had come to move. All the same it was a pretty big step we had taken, and we could imagine some of our friends back at St Ives shaking their heads doubtfully. But then – as yet none of them had seen our new home. Once seen – well it had to be seen to be believed.

Jess and I linked arms and strolled back to the house, whose lights glowed comfortingly in the distant darkness, like a beacon at sea.

'Isn't it marvellous?' I said.

*

As the days went by I had no reason to change my first, instinctive opinion. The thing about the Old Sawmills that was quite unique was, in fact, its setting, completely cut off from all the exterior trappings. Indeed, coming around the bend on the railway and seeing it suddenly laid out, like a scene from a picture, it looked what it was, very much a world of its own. I never tired of pausing on the railway track and taking in the breath-taking view – the pink and white cottage nestling among the trees, whose variations of green created a pattern of beauty such as any painter would have appreciated. The view was enhanced, of course, when the tide was up, reflecting the pastoral scene like a gigantic mirror ... and the finishing touch was put by the daily appearance of two graceful swans who appeared to look on our creek as their private possession, and viewed in cold disdain the grumpy growling of Taffy, our very neurotic Welsh sheep-dog, who did not quite know what to make of the transition from the surfing beach of Porthmeor to this quiet backwater.

Still, though the view might be placid, life was unlikely to be so for some considerable time. In the first place, living in such an isolated place meant a great deal of coming and going, and whenever possible, of course, we made these journeys by boat. Originally we had imagined using one of the three boats which had been left, but we discovered that each of them required attention of some sort. So, for the time being we found ourselves relying mainly on our old Zodiac which, being virtually unsinkable and (more important perhaps) untippable, proved surprisingly adaptable for carrying quite large loads. During our first week at the Old Sawmills the Zodiac was to be seen zooming down river with such loads as (1) six bags of cement, (2) 35 10-feet lengths of timber, (3) a sink unit, (4) a 10 feet by 4 feet window frame, (5) a huge radiogram – not to mention endless boxes of food and other belongings.

Most of the materials were part of what might be called our First Month Plan – for the conversion of the old workshop into a large, modern kitchen. Looking back now I am sure that, if we had really understood the problems involved, we might well have jibbed at the alarming prospect. Fortunately we amateurs rushed in where perhaps professionals might have hesitated. At least the result in the end was – a new kitchen. But it wasn't quite as simple as all that …

First, we needed plenty of help. Fortunately it was the Easter holidays so we had Stephen and occasionally some of his friends, who paid week-end visits. Next our elder son, Martin, had come down from London for the summer, and was to spend a month working for us. Finally Gill and her husband Alan came down for a fortnight's holiday – for Alan, I fear, the holiday was very much a working one, as we could not resist taking advantage of his experience of building work. Although we were all enthusiastic and willing, at least Alan had some professional knowledge, and this was to get us over several awkward patches.

The first task was to pull down the old rickety floor which cut the huge workshop into two parts. If this floor had been sound we would have been saved a lot of trouble, but it just wasn't so

– indeed several times while up there throwing down a mass of rubbish Martin and I nearly went through the rotting planks. We had quite a morning breaking things up, and in a surprisingly short space of time the vast area was reduced to its original empty shell.

Now we had to begin laying the beams for the new floor. This meant hacking out large holes in the walls at two-foot intervals. If the walls had been solid granite we probably could never have managed, but fortunately they had been made with local slate, packed in tight formation, and once we had opened up a space the task became straightforward, if laborious. It was a tedious business altogether, and took nearly a couple of days before Alan and Martin between them had prepared eleven holes one side and eleven the other, ready for the insertion of the very heavy 9-inch by 3-inch beams we had brought along with the furniture. Each of these beams measured 20 feet in length and required three people to lift it, so the problems involved can be imagined – especially when, after inserting several beams, we discovered the space left for manoeuvring to be decreasing alarmingly! However, in the end we had all the beams in place – and Alan and Martin began the even more tortuous business of clambering about with a leveller and wedges, getting everything levelled up.

All this took several days, and Jess began to despair – even so she was pleasantly surprised, on returning from three days at the pottery, to find the entire planking laid and a floor of 22 by 18 feet waiting for the final touch of a good sealing.

It was quite an achievement, and we celebrated it with a family dinner and some Anjou Rosé – a favourite drink of all of us after our boating trips to France. It was quite an occasion with so many members of the family, usually scattered, sitting around the table. Gill married and living in London; Jane working in Wardour Street; Demelza at a drama school; Martin with a wine firm; now Stephen a weekly lodger at St Ives and Genevieve soon to be a weekly boarder at Penzance – this was to be a far cry from the early days of St Christopher's when eight of us sat down to every meal. Well, I had to admit that physically Jess and I would welcome a change from endlessly cooking for such a large family. We felt ready for a period of peace and calm up our little creek – an experience, we felt too, that would render all the more enjoyable these occasional family get-togethers.

Our celebration dinner only marked a momentary lull in the relentless building operations. Having put down the floor, what about the walls? At the moment they were rough slate, and not very edifying. In the longest outer wall, anyway, we had to put a window, for there was none at all at the moment, otherwise our kitchen would be a dark and dismal place. What about the other walls? In the end we decided to whitewash the wall opposite the one which was to have a window, and to tongue and groove the other two walls with 4-inch planks.

From experience at St Christopher's I knew that I could manage the tongue and grooving quite adequately (I use the word carefully as the family opinion of the result is not entirely favourable), but the problem of inserting a large window in a slate wall of two-foot thickness presented quite a few headaches, especially as Jess insisted on having a picture-book window, so wide that it offered panoramic views of our creek. We had many anxious discussions – not the least of our worries being the fact that the kitchen was being built quite high up, so that the window had to go in a wall that was itself about 20 feet above the ground. In the end we were to realize that this was an advantage – there was less quantity of slate likely to fall down when we opened up the wall!

Fortunately Alan was still with us, and showed us how to go about digging out a first line about six inches deep in the wall, with pick-axe crowbar. Even this was quite a task, and hinted at the difficulties to come. Before we could contemplate taking away any more of the wall to put in our window we had first to insert what is known as a lintel. Sometimes these are of granite or concrete, but the weight of these was beyond consideration, so we decided on two sturdy wooden ones, 6 ins deep by 12 ins wide, and 10 feet long. Even this apparently represented a special order and the timber yard had to send away for the beams ... and getting them from Golant by boat presented quite a problem, but one which our Zodiac handled triumphantly.

At last one day Martin hacked through to let in daylight, and very gingerly we began trying to insert the first of the two lintels.

Everywhere there were little props to stop the roof caving in, and it was a most complicated task, but somehow, by a mixture of cajoling and hammering, we actually got the first (outside) lintel into place. However, when it came to inserting the second lintel ... Now we were really in trouble, for at several places the wall began crumbling. What we *should* have done of course, and no doubt a professional builder would have done it instinctively, was to have taken down the three or four feet of wall above us, put in the lintels and built up again. What we did in the end amounted to much the same, since most of the wall came away in bits and pieces ... be that as it may, the end result was – we had our two lintels proudly in place, and all ready for the insertion of our steel window frame.

And then, having fixed the window frame, there was the little matter of the glass panes – two measuring 2 feet by 2 feet, two measuring 2 feet by 1 foot, and one enormous one measuring 4 feet by 4 feet – all of which had to be transported from Golant Railway Halt by river. No wonder the locals became fascinated at our comings and goings. Mind you, it was not always possible to make use of nautical transport, for if the tide was out then the Zodiac could not reach the house. More than once, when in a desperate hurry for materials, Martin and I had to get out of the car and load on to our shoulders a dozen or so planks and march down the railway carrying them in single file procession. Normally this was rather a beautiful walk, with the gentle waters of the River Fowey ebbing below – carrying a large weight rather altered one's perspective. Besides, there was always the remote chance of one of the china clay goods trains suddenly rumbling round the bend ahead and emitting an ear-splitting blast on its horn.

No sooner had we finished the window of our new kitchen than I began lining the walls with tongue and groove. When I had done this before at St Christopher's it had been a comparatively simple matter, for there had been a wood backing. Here, with only slate walls, I found unexpected problems, and though I managed in the end, some uncomplimentary remarks were paid about the rather fragile state of my new 'wall' – still, there was so much else to do that we agreed it would pass.

In fact, the more we worked on our new kitchen, the more there seemed to be done, the longer the task took – it soon began to get really depressing. The false roof, for instance – though we had cut our workshop into two, there was still about 15 feet from our floor to the real roof, and this made the kitchen look ridiculous. We decided to make a lower roof, and this meant once again laying beams, and then fixing to them sheets of celotex, a kind of soft board. Needless to say we soon found ourselves facing dire problems, such as the unexpected sagging of the roofing material in parts where we had unthinkingly laid the beams just a little too far apart ... however, in the end, with judicious use of sticky tape to hide the joins and then a final coat of bright orange paint we finished our roof.

Unfortunately – or perhaps I should say fortunately, according to how one thinks time should be spent – our kitchen was only one of a dozen and more tasks awaiting us. I don't think I have ever worked so hard physically as during our first few months at the Old Sawmills. Jess probably worked even harder than I, for she embarked enthusiastically on a large scale gardening project, having felt starved of the land while at St Christopher's. Soon she had laid cloches, opened up the greenhouse, and turned over several patches of land. Here again we came up against the problems involved with isolation. To save time we wished to hire a rotavator – but could we get anyone to come out? One man did actually come and view, but he hummed and hawed and quoted a ridiculous price – and even so we felt in our hearts he would never come.

No, one thing being at the Old Sawmills soon taught us – just as *Sanu* had done – was that life must become more of a do-it-yourself affair. In fact this has proved very valuable experience for us all.

The next item to claim our attention was the workshop. During the building operations we had rather thoughtlessly thrown all the contents into a gigantic heap – now, with difficulty, we began tidying up. We were constantly making strange discoveries – lamps, stoves, batteries, boxes of tools, machine parts, boat propellors, even in one corner, mounted neatly on a four wheel truck, a complete Morris Ten motor car engine. And of course, everywhere, boat parts, for one of the previous owners had been a boat builder. And not merely parts, sometimes whole engines – there were several 'Seagulls.' For the time being we stacked these to one side and concentrated on clearing everything away, uncovering a marvellous 12-foot work-bench, rejuvenating the power-driven woodsaw so that we could cut up logs for the fires, and tentatively clearing a space for the pottery kiln which, one day, Jess might have time to consider using.

At last the workshop was in reasonable order, and we turned our attention to the boats. We had, we found, acquired no less than five, but one, it turned out, belonged to someone else and was duly towed away. That left four – a 12-foot motor boat, a 13-foot 6 clinker inboard boat, a 16-foot fibreglass hull, and an 11-foot dinghy. When we came to examine these more closely we found that the fibreglass hull needed extensive repairs and the clinker built boat was minus engine and needed new planks, so that left two – the 12-foot motor boat, which was of a flashy type none of us liked, and the rather pleasant little dinghy. We decided to spruce up the motor boat with a view to selling, to re-sheath the fibreglass hull, to aim one day to get the clinker boat in working order with a small inboard engine – and in the meantime to use the small dinghy and our own Zodiac. Like many projects this one has tended to remain somewhat on the drawing board and we continued running backwards and forwards on the Zodiac and the dinghy, which are really very efficient. But on the quay stands a gleaming blue and white motor boat for sale, and that fibre glass bottom *is* getting sheathed – very slowly.

Then I must not forget the houseboat, *Heron* as it was called on the sale details (four single berths with Dunlopillo mattresses, small galley with calor gas cooker, toilet with marine WC etc). For a long time this remained tucked up the creek, and then, as we began to find ourselves very short of money to continue with our plans, we decided – why not sell the houseboat? No sooner said than done, we hoped, and rushed off an advertisement to the local paper. Indeed potential customers came – all kinds of strange groups, which suggested the housing problem to be as difficult in our new area as elsewhere. Unfortunately, the houseboat was really more a week-end type of home, and most decidedly not suited to couples with four small children, who seemed the preponderance among callers.

Perhaps it was the concentration on boating that nagged us at last into fulfilling what was after all one of the main purposes of our removal to Fowey – namely, the provision of a permanent home for our dear seventh child, *Sanu*. Ever since we acquired her this had been a constant bugbear, the lack of reliable accommodation: always there was the haunting, worrying feeling that something might go wrong with one or other of the temporary berths we used. It had, indeed been rather like having an elderly relative whom nobody really wanted. First, at Falmouth, we had been very temporary guests of the Falmouth Boat Company on a mooring which was generally much in use. Then a few uncomfortable hours spent at the mercy of the ground-swell in St Ives Harbour had quickly made clear its unsuitability for it, and its unsuitability for our huge boat. The later berths in Hayle had at least offered some shelter, but we were soon moved out of the Lelant Quay, and later some extensions by Harvey's threatened our snug corner by the timber yard – we had, meantime, appealed in vain to the harbour masters of Penzance and Newlyn. No, it was a great problem, always with us …

What we had dreamed of, of course, was finding somewhere where we could, almost literally, keep *Sanu* at the bottom of the garden. Now we had just such a haven. One day we could keep her literally at our big quay, but until we had prepared the site we proposed keeping her on a mooring. The spot we had chosen, Wiseman's Pool, up the River Fowey, was an ideal one, well protected from sea and wind, and in a lovely setting with the tree-lined river reach stretching up towards Lostwithiel and Lerryn. We arranged with Toms' Boatyard of Polruan to lay us a really heavy mooring, and at last, one Saturday afternoon, we were able to bring *Sanu* out of her winter quarters at Flushing, and over to what was to be her permanent home.

As ever – in our heart of hearts, I do not think we expected otherwise – the occasion had its usual touch of drama: though not, as we half imagined, to do with the weather. In fact the weather forecast was Force 4-5, but the trip from Falmouth round to Fowey was only about 20 miles and in a boat like *Sanu* perfectly safe. We set off with rising spirits, glad to be aboard again – sobering up somewhat as we realized we were making that very same trip as the ill-fated *Darlwyn* had once made. However, once past the grim outline of Dodman Point we cheered up as we saw quite clearly the outline of Gribben Head, and what was in future to be our new home port, Fowey. Exactly three hours after leaving the berth at Flushing we were motoring slowly past Fowey Quay, alongside the big, large ships at the docks, and up to Wiseman's Pool, where all that remained to be done was to pick up our mooring. We had, I might say, taken the precaution of motoring out to look at the mooring in the Zodiac a day or two before, so that we were sure we had the right buoy in mind! – now it awaited us, with the name *Sanu* painted in bold white lettering.

Picking up a mooring, as we knew, was always likely to be somewhat 'fraught' as one of our crew termed it – if the helmsman misjudges, the person deputed to pick up the buoy with a boathook is left embarrassingly too far away, and the whole approach has to be repeated. Fortunately we had had considerable experience of this at Falmouth, and now – it was anyway dead calm in the river – I had no trouble in edging *Sanu's* snub nose quietly up to the buoy, for Stephen to lean down and haul it up in triumph ... then our unexpected trouble began. For, no doubt in response to my repeated warnings that we were a really large boat, Toms had gone and laid a mooring so heavy that she might well have done for the *Queen Mary* (or so we felt just then). Quite apart from the enormous weight below, there was a $\frac{3}{4}$ inch chain to be pulled up, even after first pulling up the mooring rope. First Stephen, then Stephen and Martin, in the end both of them, myself, Jess and Genevieve, our whole crew of that day, were tugging on the rope. We wound it round the winch and began turning the handles, but progress remained slow ... at last the huge chain made its appearance, got as far as the hawse-pipe and then stuck. Alas, we realized, the shackle joining the chain to the rope was just too big to pass through, and so we were unable to wind in the chain in the normal way.

And indeed, as we struggled and sweated and swore for the next hour, we began to think we would never get the chain aboard in any style. The truth was its deadweight was just too much to manage. On top of everything else we were due to go out that evening and time was passing alarmingly ... at last, by a superhuman effort, we managed to get six feet of the chain on to the deck and made it fast as best we could, adding on a nylon rope for safety.

It wasn't quite the smooth homecoming we had hoped for, but the next day Toms came out by launch and we fitted a $\frac{1}{2}$ inch chain on the top 18 feet so that in future we would be able to handle more easily. And then at last we were able to relax and feel that *Sanu* was home. The next morning I took a precautionary walk through the woods down to the river, and there she lay, snug and cosy in her sheltered anchorage, awaiting our pleasure for her next trip.

II

The Return of the Prodigals

Life, of course, especially with the children, is never at all as one hopefully plans. If in those early months at the Old Sawmills Jess and I had indulged in the wildest speculations these would not have included the possibility that within a couple of years instead of just us living a quiet reclusive life in our new remote home – practically the entire Val Baker family would be living there. Yet this is the quirky trick of Fate which I shall now, somewhat resignedly, recount.

It may well even have been my own fault. Soon after we had moved to the Old Sawmills, with Genevieve becoming a weekly boarder at Penzance, our famous 'family of eight' had suddenly dwindled to the two of us, the statutory patriarchal and matriarchal figures. As if even that was not enough a new contingency was introduced by the fact that though we had left the West Penwith area Jess still remained a partner in the Mask Pottery. Though she could arrange pottery affairs to suit her own convenience as much as possible this still meant that it was necessary for her to spend three days a week down at the pottery premises, now in Penzance. In short, fairly early every Wednesday morning mine was the melancholy task of walking Jess along the railway track, or taking her in the Zodiac if the tide was right, and seeing her to the car, and then waving a rather sad farewell as she drove off on the 50-mile trip down to Penzance where she would spend the next three days and two nights.

For myself, correspondingly, there was the same period of complete solitude, at the Old Sawmills. It was ironic really, for if anyone felt like a period of solitude it was especially Jess. Instead she was spending three hectic days at the pottery with

her old comrades, Jackie, June, Virginia and Shirley, staying
the couple of nights with June who had acquired a house at
Drift just on the Land's End road, and invariably enjoying
some social outing in the evenings, just as had been the custom
in our former days. Contrariwise, I, who had had a good deal
of solitude in my life at various times and was not particularly
feeling in the mood for it just now, appeared faced with a
permanent three days alone! Of course, there were things to
do, plenty of writing of my own, work on a new book about
Sanu, editing the next issue of the *Cornish Review* – and more
mundane activities like shopping in Fowey or Par or St Austell
– but in the end there came the long lonely evenings. Then,
somehow, all the romantic glory of the Old Sawmills became
shrouded with shadows that were just a little disturbing. Often
before darkness fell I used to walk down to the quay and stare
out across the water towards the main river, and think,
sometimes rather unnervingly, now I am *entirely* alone here,
miles from another human being, just me and the silent empty
world around.

Of course, the world was not really silent, but too often full
of the calls of blackbirds and rooks, and pigeons. Once I saw a
colourful kingfisher and several types of heron: so in a way you
might say I was by no means alone. But I felt alone, more
alone than ever in my life probably. And so, perhaps, who
knows, I began working subterraneously towards the
reconstitution of those family days that seemed in retrospect
such happy memories.

The first change for the better would have come anyway, for
Jess now found the Penzance arrangement far too strenuous
altogether. After about a year of shilly-shallying she managed
to sell her share of the Mask Pottery, so that she was no longer
forced to depart for those three days a week. It had always been
her intention eventually to start a small pottery of her own up
at the Old Sawmills, but for the moment it was early spring
and time for her to indulge her great love of gardening. With
spasmodic aid from me, an unwilling gardener, she cleared a
space up in the woods and soon had laid beds of lettuce, peas,
beans, beetroot, and so on. In fact for a while I probably saw
less of her than before – but at least we were together again,

and things seemed as the northerners have a nice way of putting it, 'proper.'

The next thing was that we found we simply could not manage any longer to meet the vastly increased school fees for Genevieve's weekly boarding school at Penzance. She was fifteen now, anyway, and so would be eligible for the local tech – and so she gave up her old routine and became a student at the Local Technical College. I had always been a little nervous of this impending change, fearful that Genevieve would be lonely, would find the walk along the railway track too depressing, and so on and so forth ... Jess, wiser in her motherhood, said don't worry, she'll soon make friends. And of course in no time it seemed Genevieve had struck up several local friendships, and was even being given lifts back from St Austell every day from some kindly Golant driver.

By now our other children were scattered far and wide: Stephen had gone to Leeds University on a botany course, Martin was driving a delivery van for a wine firm in the West End of London, Jane was film editing in Soho, Gill was married and living at Surbiton with her husband Alan and her very pretty spastic baby, Emily; and Demelza – well, Demelza had been pursuing her usual dramatic deviations. When it had become apparent some years before that Demelza's academic career was hardly likely to be an impressive one (her main achievement at her school being to have absconded with the school bell) we hunted around for the best way of exploiting what talents she had. These were, briefly – acting and selling. (This latter ability we knew well from exploits in our own pottery shop.) However, acting was what Demelza really wanted to do, so cap in hand we went up to London, saw Ruth Conti, delightful head of the famous Italia-Conti Drama School, and enrolled Demelza as a pupil. It was rather early in her life, she was still only fifteen, but it was a fact that the school had pupils from eleven upwards, and we reckoned she could have a room at Surbiton with her elder sister, Gill.

Of course, things didn't work out as planned! Although Demelza obviously did have a very real talent for drama, she lacked concentration, and after a year there seemed no point, either to the school or to us, in her continuing. While we all tried to make some sensible decision about her future, Demelza loyally took a few jobs in boutiques and shoe shops to earn her own living. Then one night the phone rang in Fowey, and a babbling excited voice came on to introduce us to the strange tale of Demelza, the Busker's Bottler.

What had happened was this. Chatting with a crowd of fellow teenagers in Soho Demelza learned that 'Jumping Jack' was needing a 'Bottler.' Why didn't she go down to Leicester Square and see him there and then? Up to that point she had no idea what a bottler was or even who or what Jumping Jack might be, but being Demelza she gaily set off down to Leicester Square, where she found a fairly elderly gentleman with various musical instruments entertaining a waiting cinema queue. In fact the musical instruments were not vastly in use, as most of Jumping Jack's repertoire consisted of tap dancing, hence his nickname. As for the bottling part, Jumping Jack explained this pithily to Demelza during a break in his performance. He was the busker, she would be the bottler. He gave the crowd their entertainment, her job would be to go along the line collecting the financial reward. It was not exactly easy, but she was welcome to have a try, and she could keep a third of whatever money she took.

Thus began Demelza's extraordinary new career, which lasted for nearly six months, from the golden days of late summer through autumn and right up to a snowy, wintry but amazingly profitable Christmas. With Jumping Jack, an aged old gentleman who wore flapping clothes, Demelza must have made an odd contrast, but during the few weeks they worked together she learned her new trade well. Apparently Jumping Jack was something of a legend in the busking world, so that Demelza was lucky to have the advantage of working with him. This work, by the way, involved strange fields and by-ways as far as busking went – most buskers stayed around the West End, but Jumping Jack had odd beats of his own, one of them being the Stock Exchange at mid-day.

We would dearly have loved to have seen Demelza and Jumping Jack at work, but by the time we were able to get to London and see for ourselves Demelza had found, as apparently others did before her, that Jumping Jack was a difficult man to work for. She passed on to team up with 'The One-Man Band,' an experienced younger busker whose act consisted of playing a huge drum tied to his back, banging a cymbal, playing a guitar and, I think, blowing a mouthorgan, all at the same time. We didn't know it then but he had a wife and two small children and lived perfectly normally somewhere in a suburban home ... but to see him standing on the pavement dressed in way-out beatnik outfit and a large straw hat, and bearing his paraphernalia of musical instruments you might have thought him a creature from outer space (and Demelza a suitable companion, in a sombrero hat and dark maxi-trousers). However, they apparently made a good combination and in no time had worked out a regular routine of spending about twenty minutes at each of several nearby cinema queues, The Leicester Square. Empire and the Odeon Cinema in Leicester Square, The Plaza and the Carlton in Haymarket. During this twenty minutes, The One Man Band performed while walking slowly up and down the queue (something to do with police regulations, I fancy). Demelza for her part passed up and down the queue in a more intimate and purposeful way, collecting the lolly.

We only saw Demelza in action on one occasion, but it was enough to explain her extraordinary success in this new vocation. It was outside the Carlton Cinema, where a new Peter Cook and Dudley Moore film ensured a nice long queue. While the valiant One-Man Band was blaring and bumping away Demelza was – no, not passing politely alongside the queue – but actually working her way *through it.* To put it more succinctly, she was standing four-square in front of each member of the queue, holding out her bottle (actually, ironically, a Midland Bank money bag) – and really the poor people weren't given much chance. I feel sure that if forcibly approached in such circumstances I would probably have refused to give a penny, but apparently this seldom happened. If anyone did have the temerity to object Demelza launched into a harangue about how lucky the person was to have the *privilege* of listening to such a talented artist – and did they realise artists had to eat, etc! It was seldom that the coins weren't produced and clinked down into the magic bag.

Of course it wasn't for us to enter too closely into Demelza's new world, but I must say it sounded rather fascinating. The buskers had formed themselves into a sort of unofficial closed shop – there were probably only a few dozen in all – and they had their regular code. One of the recognised rules was that you didn't 'top' another busker – i.e. if someone was already playing a queue, you didn't try and start above him and cut into his profits; presumably you waited until he had finished and moved on. At that time there didn't seem to be any serious disagreements, and I was not surprised for apparently they were all collecting in quite large sums of cash every day. Demelza herself had days when she collected £10 in 10 minutes and as Christmas time approached these figures went up and up ... reaching a record of £25 in one half hour period. Of course there were disadvantages, it has to be remembered. It was cold standing in the London streets in November and December – and the police were not friendly, always moving them on and often threatening. All the same there was a cheerful friendliness about the buskers in their regular meeting place, the Earl of Leicester Pub in Museum Square where in between performances they cleaned their guitars and drums and trumpets in one corner and planned new strategies.

It wasn't, of course, one could see, a career of any real permanance (though I was fascinated to find that several buskers often went off to the Continent to busk around France or Spain or Holland, as a break) and anyway there was always the background criminal element of Soho to make one feel a little uneasy. It seemed to us that Demelza was beginning to look more and more tired and washed out, and so we began dropping gentle hints that it might do her good to come down to Cornwall for a while. We didn't really expect these to get any response, but lo and behold one day in the next frosty January I found myself standing on Par Station waiting to welcome a much taller Maxi-skirted figure with about five suitcases and a couple of guitars. A second child was home ...

The idea at the time was that Demelza would come down more or less for an extended holiday, and I must say the fresh

Cornish air soon put colour back in her cheeks. But as week after week went by we began to realise that somehow she wasn't really so keen to go back to the grimy city. At first she thought she might pick up a local job, but at about this time there came a new development – Jess and I heard of a former painting studio and pottery premises for sale in Fowey itself, and suddenly thought that there might be some sense in acquiring this, and thus obtaining for ourselves a direct retail outlet, where, of course, the services of our star saleswoman of the family would be invaluable. So we came to be busy for several weeks re-decorating our latest venture, the Wheelcat Pottery at 19, North Street, in the heart of 'Q's' Troy Town. The premises as such consisted of a workroom on one floor, with a tiny kitchen and toilet and small store room: and above it, rather surprisingly a more gracious long low studio room, with windows all round allowing light to pour in. Behind there were the usual arrangements common to that part of Fowey – tier after tier of garden plots rising up against the granite background, though all now wild and overgrown.

Someday we decided we must make the gardens attractive, but for the moment common sense diverted resolute attention on turning the old workroom into a pottery shop. This was not too difficult, in fact; mostly a coat of white paint all round, and then erection of lots of shelving, plus the knocking down of a small partition wall in order to make room for a pottery kiln and wheel. Before long we had laid a plain Chinese carpet, and filled the shelves with colourful new orange and red and green glazed pots – and the shop was literally ready for business, with Demelza installed at a small table, eagerly awaiting her first customers.

There still remained the problem of what to do with the nice room upstairs. It was almost big enough to be a small theatre, and our mind played with such ideas as running a folk club – however, in the end we decided to try out the idea of a small art gallery, showing a variety of paintings by local artists. As soon as word had been passed round we began having visitors, shyly (sometimes not so shyly!) presenting their work. We managed in the end to assemble about 60 paintings including a few by

friends like Margo Maeckleberghe and Peter Liddle and Lionel
Miskin who were quite well known. Meantime, I rushed round
buying eight by four sheets of chipboard, painting them white,
lining the ceiling of the studio, and setting up one or two angle
walls. It was all rather exhausting – and was in fact to prove rather
disappointing – but at least it made an attractive show. And in
the meantime, Demelza was showing she had not lost her art of
salesmanship in the pottery shop, which at least appeared like to
make economic sense.

While this was going on, inexorably the return of the prodigals was continuing. For some years now our eldest, Martin after
walking out of Hornsey Art School in despair and thus throwing
away the chance of an interesting career – had retired into a
peculiar life of working the summer season down in his beloved
St Ives, where he could always get a job in a café, and the winters
in London, where he usually picked up a driving job for one of
the wine companies. It was a life that often filled us with a sense
of despair, but it was Martin's choice, and he seemed content to
go along like this. Indeed often we had the terrifying feeling he
would still be doing this when he was fifty or sixty. During his
winter in London he would rent some incredibly small room,
always in the Fulham area which he liked – one room, I think
measured ten feet by seven feet across. We never quite knew why
but Martin seemed to have a genius for becoming involved with
eccentric landladies – including one rather marvellous one who
finally, after not allowing him to use a bathroom, or even to
cook, I believe, conceived a fantasy that he had been sent by MI5
to spy upon her! However, as protection against all these
annoyances Martin had developed an almost obsessive interest
in tape recording, with a large modern tape recorder on which
he taped hundred of old jazz records, folk songs and so forth. In
his younger days he had been very involved with CND, Com-
mittee of 100 and so on, and he still mixed a lot with friends of
that circle, but somehow he seemed to be retired somewhat into
a world of his own.

Which made it all the more surprising and pleasant for us to
hear that this spring Martin was *not* going to make his usual
pilgrimage from Porthmeor to London, but thought he might

come down to the Old Sawmills for a while. As a matter of fact, he wrote (in one of his bi-annual letters) he had been thinking quite a lot about the dam we had thought of constructing across the centre of our creek, so as to create a permanent lake. Well, he enclosed a few diagrams to show his ideas. Perhaps he could come and work for a couple of weeks in return for his keep? Then later he would look round for a job.

True to his promise, Martin arrived and immediately embarked on the seemingly Herculean task of building up the remnants of the dam that had once existed. To be strictly fair, Stephen and one or two of his friends had on past occasions, rather spasmodically, piled up large stones and slates to construct the basis of part of the dam. But now with what for him seemed to Jess and me quite alarming energy Martin spent day after day ferrying boatloads of heavy stones from one end of the valley down to the dam site. Considering that like me he cannot swim, his method seemed highly dangerous, as it involved over loading a notoriously unstable old sailing dinghy and then tipping the stones over while afloat. Later, when the tide had gone out, he would don wellingtons and manhandle the stones into position. In this manner, day by day the dam wall began to extend further and further – that is to say, nearer and nearer to our quay on the opposite side. Eventually, when there was just a few feet of space left, the idea was to build a sluice gate, so that we could control the water, and occasionally empty our new artificial lake.

I must say Martin's enthusiasm was commendable, even though it meant that he was unable to spare time for the work which I really would have preferred, namely cutting us a huge batch of wood logs ready for our winter period. And it was certainly exciting to watch the dam grow and grow – and not only the dam, either, for by some quirk three or four huge tree trunks, which Stephen had cut down and planted as stakes, in order to strengthen the dam walls, had actually sprouted leaves. However, soon Martin's pecuniary circumstances made it imperative for him to find a job. This, one would have thought fairly easy, in the late spring in Cornwall, but it was not to prove so. As Martin had worked extremely hard for many years up till then, it made him – and us – a little angry when he had the greatest difficulty in obtaining any kind of sympathetic attention from the local Ministry of Labour and Security (the old idea that state security is some kind of charity benevolently doled out dies very hard). Under the present laws of the country the working people more than pay for any assistance, such as unemployment or insurance money which they may need – but too often this is not reflected in the supercilious attitude of employment exchange staffs.

In the end, entirely through his own efforts, Martin obtained a job driving for a local furniture firm – one which owing to our remote position meant rising at 6 am, a walk along the railway track to Fowey, then a long bus journey into St Austell. So all at once, after having got used to seeing Martin around at all times of the day and night, suddenly we never saw Martin at all, for from the beginning his hours of work seemed to include much overtime.

By now, however, yet another of the prodigals was back, though we had to greet his return with mixed feelings. Stephen had always been our one academically brainy child, and for Jess in particular, who went herself to university and held the academic world in great veneration, it was very important that Stephen, at least, should fulfil his educational potential. Even I could see the sense of this – once he had passed through university and obtained a degree and so forth, then the world would be largely at his feet – for instance he could go in to marine biology, a fascinating subject.

Nearly a year ago we had stood on King's Cross Station at midnight and waved farewell to our son, off to his new life at Leeds University: since then he had soon settled in to the social whirl, and after a few rows with landladies found a pleasant niche sharing a flat with several other students, including a friend from Penzance. Now and then he would make the usual long distance reverse charge call that has long been a feature of our family life, and we gathered that *socially* life was fine. And work … ? Often, too often, there was an uncomfortable silence.

Now gradually it all emerged: Stephen had failed his exams and his university career was at an abrupt end; but more than that, he was not even sorry. He had entered the anarchist phase which besets so many students, as a result of which all the establishment – universities, schools, politics – even us, in many ways – were condemned. What did he want to do then? He just wanted to *Live*. So he had come home, of course. But he quite realised he would have to get a job, indeed he *wanted* a job where he could use his body rather than his brain – a period of manual labour would do him good.

In point of fact Stephen is fit as a fiddle, and very strong – and indeed, we wished we could afford to employ him doing all kinds of odd jobs around the Old Sawmills, but we just couldn't. However, for a few brief weeks somehow Stephen managed to exist ... and during that period he applied himself with renewed enthusiasm to his Monument. Perhaps I should explain here that since we came to the Old Sawmills we have all acquired our own private monuments of one sort or another. Mine has been our broken down quay on the main river; Martin's has been an old Commer van that has stood for weeks in the lane at Golant awaiting a method of working the gears: Jess's – well, she would deny it, but to a large extent it has been her plot, on which she has laboured for so many hours only to be frustrated by rats, a large pig, field mice, and other hazards.

For Stephen, his monument from beginning to end has been The Tractor. It was here when we came, and I am sure it will be here when we are gone, and in much the same general condition. When we first surveyed the enticing sales details of the Old Sawmills, that tractor was a particularly juicy item: 'Bristol 22 Diesel Crawler Tractor, complete with hydraulics and bulldozer blade, large rear transport box, etc.' Oh, I remember it well. It stood in those days somewhere up in the woods, and the owner explained quite enthusiastically his plans *one day,* for using it to build a road that would require a total distance of nearly two miles to reach the nearest highway.

At the time we were impressed by the idea of casually acquiring a caterpillar tractor as we were by many other items, such as an old motor cruiser and a houseboat, both of which came to watery grief – but I personally never had much faith or hope in it. Stephen however, seemed to look on it as a personal challenge, and over all the months of his school holidays and whenever he could get any spare time he would work on that tractor. Frequently he would invite friends down from Penzance for the weekend, ostensibly to help (an expensive process for us as we not only had to feed them but usually take them out for a Saturday night drink as well). Now whereas I was against the whole project from the start, unfortunately Jess, as yet not fully disillusioned by Stephen's impending academic abandonment, took an indulgent and for her costly view. She it was who paid for item after item – a new starter, a new rotator, a new battery (and another new battery later) – finally our immensely expensive operation of new track rods and heaven knows what. I, of course, made plenty of ironic cracks, but these probably did more harm than good.

All this had gone on and on and on ... and in fact all that the tractor had ever achieved, even when finally one day to everyone's amazement its old diesel engine broke into wheezy song, was (a) to dig a refuse heap, (b) to dig it over again, (c) to tear up some perfectly sound and useful drains, damaging the pipes so that we had to spend £20 buying some new ones. And time went on and on ... and now here was Stephen not only thrown out of university, but back in the Old Sawmills, free to concentrate almost entirely for a while upon his beloved monument.

I must say he worked hard and long hours getting it going, and the day came quite soon when it roared up and down the far bed of the creek. Obviously it wasn't doing much good there, so Stephen decided to move further down the creek with the fairly rational idea of trying to deepen the channel from the main river. Apparently he went on just a little too far, with the result that at a particularly sharp and muddy bend in the river bed – the tractor became stuck. Well and truly stuck – and not only stuck, but even began to sink into the oozy mud.

This was, it transpired, to prove a fatal situation, for already the tide was beginning to come up Fowey River. Soon, too soon, the water would begin to fill up our little creek, as surely on this day as on every other day (twice daily to be exact). And just as surely the embedded tractor would be not merely awash, but completely submerged.

All this I could see at a glance, merely by looking out of our kitchen window upon the depressing sight of that damned tractor, already half under the mud, with Stephen and Jess and a couple of others frantically trying to perform miracles with levers and so forth. I *knew* (one always knows where other people's monuments are concerned!) that nothing could stop the time and tide, etc.

And so, of course, it happened ... eventually the humans had to retreat, after stuffing packing in the exhaust pipe, leaving the poor old tractor to be swallowed up.

And that, you might have thought, would be that. But by no means. The tide came in, the tide went out – the tide came in again, the tide went out again – the tractor and all its vital organs was very wet indeed. However, if only she could be got out, even now ... Suddenly there appeared the blond, rather smug figure of Genevieve, having just walked back along the railway line.

'Oh, did I tell you? – the railway men will get your tractor out for you. They'll be along in a minute.'

Incredible as it might have sounded – and did – this was precisely what happened. Along came one of the busy diesel engines that tow the china clay trucks past the end of our creek to the main docks at Fowey – only this time the engine stopped, and two men in overalls appeared to survey the scene. Stephen hastened over for a conference, then disappeared in our dinghy to fetch some wire rope and chain from *Sanu*.

Before long, rescue operations were in progress. However, as was to be expected with any monument, there were hitches. There was difficulty in getting the wire adequately attached – then the rope broke, and even the chain came apart ... all this took time, and in fact the tide came in again and operations had to cease.

However, the next morning the men were back – in fact *two* lots, for it transpired that the British Railways drivers had competed for Genevieve's favours from English China Clay drivers, who also handled locomotives – indeed there was quite an argy-bargy about which engine and which 'brand' of drivers should have the honour. I was never quite sure who won, but I know that, incredibly, when I returned from a trip to St Austell

– there was the tractor back again on safe dry land!

I would like to be able to say that there was a happy ending to the story, but with anything connected with Stephen, things are never so simple. In fact, of course, the tractor was pretty badly disabled, and Stephen could hardly begin to put things right. However there now appeared on the scene one Barney, somehow typical of a whole string of strange beings who appear in our lives at moments of crisis. Barney, who just happened to be taking a walk along the railway line, turned out to be a mechanic who knew all about tractors. The next thing we knew, he and Stephen were spending mysterious hours and hours burrowing into the tractor's suddenly exposed innards. This seemed to go on for days – weeks – months. Every now and then the engine would miraculously roar into life – But alas, there seemed to be some detail wrong. We were naturally somewhat worried about how Barney was going to be recompensed for all the time he was spending, but Stephen told us not to worry. It turned out he had worked out some complicated scheme by which he was going to join with Barney in excavating some old iron pipes on our land, and sell them for scrap, and Barney would be paid off out of that ... It all sounded almost conceivable, but somehow I couldn't help wondering ... and wondering ... and today as I write, many months, perhaps years later, there the tractor still stands, that proud old monument.

Stephen's monument was not his only interest at the Old Sawmills. Stephen actually had his own chalet (readers may remember earlier stories of Stephen's Attic). It was a cosy little chalet tucked into the granite sides of the creek, and Stephen had laboured muchly upon it, painting the walls of his bedroom a very striking with-it orange and black (once there had been a tree growing in the middle of the floor, but that fortunately went in some sudden upheaval). It was the sort of chalet in which a person could have lived quite comfortably, but we found that Stephen preferred simply to sleep there, and have occasional parties there ... for the rest, i.e. for meals, television, comforts – he preferred to come to our house. What was more, only too often, Stephen would bring with him friends – not just one, but two or three, (he had never seemed

able to throw off this expensive habit of St Christopher's days).
We were, of course, suitably touched to see they were usually
the same friends – the Nickeys, the Olivers, the Michaels, the
Pauls – but now they were all very large and tended to eat a
lot. Altogether, one way and another we were finding the
return of this particular prodigal rather exhausting and costly.

Meantime, there was yet another return, our eldest
daughter, Gill, and her little Emily. True this would appear to
be a temporary return, for Gill had merely come down for a
few summer weeks while her husband Alan was in process of
finding them a new home ... but somehow our experience has
been that nothing is so elastic as the word temporary. However
Gill possessed a great asset not notably present among most of
our other 'lodgers' – she was older and wiser and altogether
more sensible and practical about the hard everyday facts of
life. While the others might look and wonder and contemplate
various actions to be taken, Gill would get on with the job.

This is an aspect that has always especially won her Jess's
approval and so now, indeed, Gill was able immediately to give
her mother a helping hand in the little pottery workshop next
to our huge cellar. Day after day during the hot summer weeks
Gill would settle Emily in her special chair in the garden, and
then she and Jess would work in the little pottery with the door
wide open – Jess throwing mugs and vases and bowls, and Gill
doing some fettling or decorating. Gill herself made some
rather lovely pottery rings and also turned out to be rather
adept at decorating large pottery plates. This was a period
when we experimented with plates and plaques, bringing in
each of the children to try their hands at decorations. Martin
did a curious cartoon type of face – Genevieve a lush,
humorous backside of an elephant, Demelza a surrealist-cum-
abstract design. The only trouble with these plates was that
often if not dried extremely carefully they might blow up, or at
least crack. After a while all over the house there would stand
rather sad reminders – some of the most fearsome being some
plates which Genevieve whimsically decorated with a set of
human teeth.

Gill was especially quick with the sewing machine, and
under her influence Jess occasionally embarked spasmodically

on some dressmaking. Then again, the two of them would develop sudden 'brilliant' new money making ideas. One Sunday they worked like slaves putting into practice the latest bright idea. Jess had bought several yards of coloured canvas and eyelets and string, and now she and Gill, using the sewing machine, embarked on a programme of making attractive holiday bags. At the end of a long, very hard, working day they had actually made 24 finished bags, and these were promptly put up for show in the pottery shop in Fowey. They looked very pretty and I think two actually sold over a period of some weeks – but they were hardly the fortune-making scheme that had been planned.

Another of Gill's more mature assets which we now welcomed was the ability to cook. To be fair all of our family have *had* to develop this ability, but like all abilities its quality varies considerably. Now there were so many of us that, somewhat bemusedly, Jess and I came to the conclusion that the only thing to do was to behave as we did when the family was holidaying on *Sanu,* and introduced a cooking and washing up rota. So there it was – Gill cooking Sunday, Jess Monday, Denys Tuesday, Demelza Wednesday, Stephen Thursday, Genevieve Friday, Martin Saturday ... perhaps I had better not dwell too exactly upon the variations of standards, but shall I say that personal characteristics played their part. Demelza for instance would arrive home in a foul temper, rush around at great speed and finally produce a reasonably edible curry. Stephen would be much more leisurely, too leisurely by far, so that we were all half starved by the time the meal finally arrived. Martin had no interest in cooking (or alas it appeared at that time in almost anything) so that it was only safe to leave to him the sausages and chips menu. Genevieve, rather surprisingly, was quite efficient, though it is true she usually played safe with salad.

Perhaps it is time now to return to Genevieve, for this was the long summer holiday time and she, too, had become one of the workers. Seeing an evening job advertised as waitress in one of the posh Fowey hotels she agreed nervously to go along – and in no time had settled into the routine of serving hotel meals to large numbers of holiday-makers (divided by her and

her fellow waitresses into 'resies' or 'chancers,' a rather nice
terminology I always thought). As at the same time Demelza
was also usually in Fowey having worked in our pottery shop,
and Stephen and Martin invariably popped in for an evening
drink, this meant that though Genevieve did not finish work
until quite late, she did not have to face the long walk home
along the river alone. It *was* quite a long walk, too, involving
following through the docks, and then around past Wiseman's
Pool to the Old Sawmills, taking at least half an hour – but in a
crowd of three or four, a bit merry from drinking, singing
away, it became good fun.

   Yes, I had to admit, sometimes rather sourly, our children
had disproved my theories, they had undoubtedly developed
quite a busy social life in Fowey, which had always seemed to
me rather a dead sort of place. In part this life had been helped
a good deal by our opening a little pottery shop in North
Street. The shop went well enough, the gallery never seemed to
click, but the place as a whole, naturally enough, soon formed
something of a meeting place for the younger crowd of Fowey,
who were always dropping in for a chat with Demelza or with
Janet Starr, who did the throwing and pottery decoration.
Janet's husband, Tony, who helped us to generally jazz up the
premises, supplied us with line drawings for sale – someone
else brought in wooden carvings – so it went on. When the
children were not nattering away at the pottery they would be
down at the King of Prussia or the Galleon, and sometimes Jess
and I would join them, enjoying the babel of bright
conversation in moderation – but glad to creep away from the
eventual barbecue or party of some sort.

   In the shop itself, Demelza was proving a mixed blessing – a
marvellous seller, but a tyrant to be in charge. We hardly felt
we could enter our own shop without her permission, and
Janet was only allowed out grudgingly. This is always the price
one seems to have to pay for some ability in one direction,
some glaring fault in another. By the end of the season, much
as we might love her, Jess and I were vowing we would never
again employ Demelza (so joining, I suspect, a long list of
rueful employers).

   But Demelza had that other unsubduable side to her which

so often brought surprises – now suddenly she got us all
involved with one of those doomed little local ventures (at least
they always seem doomed in Cornwall). This was the Fowey
theatre, a group of young actors and actresses who took over
the Fowey Town Hall to present summer rep. There were a
dozen or so of them, and soon Demelza had taken them under
her wing, and was bringing them out to borrow props for their
shows. In the end her own theatre love was revived, and she
joined in some of their late night reviews and 'Drag' shows.
Having once, some twenty years before, come to Cornwall with
a rep company my heart bled for these young enthusiasts, for
in Cornwall as I say, such ventures always come to grief. The
local people will flock to support their amateur operatic
society's annual spree, but as for supporting professional
drama, not a hope. And now in Fowey, so it proved to be.
Although the company put on several lively productions – in a
setting like the Old Town Hall, whose dismal depressing
appearance hardly warranted the £3 a night fee they had to pay
– they quickly lost their money, and had to call off in
mid-August.

Oddly enough, that was a marvellous summer, the one of
the Return of the Prodigals. The sun, it seemed, shone every
day and our greatly swollen and re-united family was
sufficiently scattered during the week to make Sunday together
a pleasant occasion, usually sitting out on the quay eating a
bread and cheese lunch, perhaps joined by one or two friends
who had walked out from Fowey. I could see, a little uneasily,
that the Old Sawmills might well switch from being a place of
great loneliness and isolation to the other extreme, a
ceaselessly lively and occupied 'pad' of the young. Was this
exactly what Jess and I wanted? I was not sure of my own
feelings, perhaps better the company of the lively young than
merely ghosts of the past – but I could see that Jess was
beginning to feel fed up with the general strain. Unlike her I
felt I knew by instinct that things would not remain like this for
too long, there was bound to be changes and gradually
everybody would go their own ways.

And in the meantime there were many marvellous evenings,
like those Saturdays nights when we would pile into that good

old faithful servant, the inflatable Zodiac, and roar down river and over to our favourite pub in the district, the Russell at Polruan, run by Edith and Jock: Edith a stout and kindly Cornishwoman who unlike so many landlords welcomed the young with open arms and made us all at home – Jock a sweet-tempered, long-suffering man who awaited his retirement eagerly, but went on holding things together efficiently. For a time Gill helped behind the bar at the Russell, too, which made an added incentive for us all to visit there. Naturally enough the children would entice their own friends from Fowey to come across on the little ferry boat, and sometimes I would look round and see a vast crowd of them, seeming to occupy half the pub ... At such times, watching them all laughing and chattering away bright-eyed, it was impossible not to marvel at the young, the flowers coming to bloom – if only they knew how fortunate they were! Alas, by the time experience has taught them that lesson they will be with us, the elderly ones, leaning on the bar counter and drinking thoughtfully our farewell drinks ...

And then it would be back to the Zodiac, a little merry perhaps (but no matter as there are, fortunately, no breathyliser hounds watching over river traffic). It would be dark, of course, but this might be one of those heaven-sent nights when a full moon hung low in the sky behind Polruan – and by its bright light we would head the Zodiac homewards, past the anchor lights of yachts in Polruan Reach, past the bright lights of Fowey town – on and on, past long lines of huge cargo boats moored at the clay docks, and finally round the bend to Wiseman's Pool, where *Sanu* rested peacefully at slumber, awaiting her next voyage – on and on until we came to the string of fairy lights we had erected to light the quay up to the house ... Yes, these are the magic times one tends to remember, when literally the whole Val Baker family (even Jane, down on holiday from her film editing job in London) has been in one boat, flashing through the water, leaving a bright and phosphorescent wake – and of course, need I say, in all senses of the words, heading right up the creek.

Epilogue

by
Jess Val Baker

Since Denys wrote this book over ten years have passed. We left the Old Sawmills and now live in the Penberth Valley in an old mill house mentioned in the Doomsday Book. The mill wheel which once used to grind the local corn has been renovated and now turns an alternator to provide free electricity. An old ram pump pumps water high up to a tank which feed various chalets in which various members of the family live.

The children are no longer children, the teenagers have grown up and had children of their own but the family is still together and most of them live in Cornwall.

Martin is now a self-employed printer in Penzance. He also helps to run and sometimes writes for a monthly alternative newspaper, *The Peninsula Voice*. This lively paper examines controversial local issues and also looks at the effect of national policies on the county. It is well subscribed to and eagerly read and as someone says, 'it gets better and better.'

Martin is also the local impresario. I think myself that he is a frustrated musician for though he does not play an instrument he is deeply involved in music. He puts on local bands mostly at a financial loss to himself and is the manager of his sister Demelza's band Zambula, promoting them and booking their gigs.

Gill married her Liverpool boyfriend Alan and they settled in London where Alan is an art teacher and an accomplished painter. Their first child Emmy now 20, suffered severe brain damage at birth, and is mentally and physically handicapped. Gill and Alan devoted the next ten years to looking after her but in the end the task became too much for Gill's health and Emmy is now cared for in hospital, though she still spends many holidays with them. Gill also studied ceramics and is a qualified teacher in the area and a very good potter. She now has two more children, Amber aged eight and Cherry aged five, who give her great joy. They all spend most of their summers in Cornwall.

Jane was one of the more career-minded of our children. She moved on from Wardour Street to become first an assistant, and then full film editor for BBC television. Her work is mainly with documentaries. She has edited many of the BBC 2 *Forty Minutes* series and her work is widely acclaimed. She is married to Rick, a primary school teacher, and they have a boy Ben aged thirteen and a girl Lamorna aged six. They often spend summers at the Mill House.

Stephen the eldest of Denys and my children, has spent the last ten years alternatively living in America and Cornwall. He is married to Gina who comes from Minnesota and is a very good dancer. They have a boy and a girl, Paris aged ten and Amira aged six. The Mill House has been transformed by Stephen's building skills and he is also a wonderful pianist as well as playing the guitar and singing. He has his own band now, the Sunshine Blues Band, who play regularly in venues around Cornwall and further afield. He and his family presently live in a chalet at the Mill House but my hunch is that he will eventually settle in America.

Demelza, after spending some time in London, has now settled in St Just with her small son Morgan aged two ... She is a brilliant conga player and for the last three years has been playing with the best loved local Afro Rock band Zambula who hope to hit the big times one day.

And now last of all we come to Genevieve who has been living with her daughter Megan, aged four, at a chalet in the Mill House for the last few years. She makes beautiful hand decorated pottery plates and tile paintings but in this time of recession finds the marketing of them very difficult. She also plays the saxophone in Stephen's blues band but secretly wishes to sail away into the sunset. To this end she has studied for and gained her yachtmaster's certificate.

*

Denys Val Baker died on 6 July, 1984. We sat with him in turns on that last long night and into that last grey dawn.

We gathered round his body where he lay like a king, his beautiful hair brushed and flowing, his brow uncreased.

We were all there, his wife, his children, their husbands and wives and their children.

We put flowers on his breast and we kissed his cold cheek. We could not believe it and we cried without end. He was the rock on which we all leaned and nothing can ever be the same without him.

J.V.B.